Table of Contents

Introduction 6
Overview of the Book 6
Why Burgers? 8
Approach and Methodology 10
Chapter 1: Origins and Evolution 12
Predecessors to the Burger (Early meat dishes) 12
Emergence of the Modern Burger (Development in the United States) 15
Evolution of Ingredients and Toppings 18
Influence of Immigrant Communities 21
Chapter 2: Cultural Impact 24
Burger as a Symbol of American Identity 24
Globalization and International Adaptations 27
Rituals and Traditions Surrounding Burger Consumption 30
Representation in Media and Pop Culture 33
Chapter 3: Innovation and Trends 36
Invention of the Hamburger Bun 36
Rise of Fast-Food Chains 39
Gourmet Burger Revolution 43
Sustainability and Ethical Considerations 47
Chapter 4: Iconic Burger Joints 50
Classic Diners and Drive-Ins 50
Regional Favorites and Specialty Burgers 53
Celebrity Chef-Owned Establishments 57
Legacy and Longevity of Iconic Burger Joints 60
Chapter 5: Health and Nutrition 64
Perceptions of Burger Consumption Over Time 64

Nutritional Components of Burgers 68
Health Concerns and Debates 72
Rise of Plant-Based Alternatives 76

Chapter 6: Social and Economic Impact 80
Urban Development and Burger Culture 80
Job Creation and Economic Influence 84
Burger Tourism and Travel Destinations 88
Corporate Influence and Big Burger Brands 92

Chapter 7: Culinary Techniques and Recipes 97
Choosing the Right Meat and Ingredients 97
Cooking Methods and Grilling Techniques 101
Secret Sauce Recipes and Burger Hacks 105
Signature Burgers from Around the World 109

Chapter 8: Pop Culture References 114
Burger in Film and Television 114
Advertising and Marketing Campaigns 118
Burger Merchandise and Collectibles 122
Burger Festivals and Events 126

Chapter 9: Environmental and Ethical Considerations
130
Environmental Impact of Beef Production 130
Sustainable Practices in Burger Making 135
Ethical Dilemmas Surrounding Meat Consumption 139
Future of Burgers in a Changing Climate 144

Chapter 10: Future Trends 149
Technological Innovations in Burger Making 149
Changing Consumer Preferences and Demands 154
Role of Burgers in Culinary Fusion 159

Copyright © 2024 by Evelyn G. Parker (Author)

All rights reserved. This book or any portion thereof may not be reproduced or used in any manner whatsoever without the express written permission of the publisher except for the use of brief quotations in a book review.

This book is copyright protected. This is only for personal use. You cannot amend, distributor, sell, use, quote or paraphrase any part or the content within this book without the consent of the author.

Please note the information contained within this document is for educational and entertainment purposes only. Every attempt has been made to provide accurate, up to date and reliable complete information. No warranties of any kind are expressed or implied. Readers acknowledge that the author is not engaging in the rendering of legal, financial, medical or professional advice. The content of this book has been derived from various sources. Please consult a licensed professional before attempting any techniques outlined in this book.

By reading this document, the readers agree that under no circumstances are the author responsible for any losses, direct or indirect, which are incurred as a result of the use of information contained within this document, including but not limited to errors, omissions or inaccuracies.

Thank you very much for reading this book.

Title: Burgeropolis: A Culinary Expedition Through the World of Burgers
Subtitle: From Classic Creations to Cutting-Edge Cuisine - Exploring Burger Culture Worldwide

Author: Evelyn G. Parker

Predictions for the Future of Burger Culture 163
Conclusion 168
Recap of Key Themes and Insights 168
Reflections on the Journey of Exploring Burger History 171
Looking Ahead: The Enduring Legacy of the Burger 174
Glossary 178
Potential References 180

Introduction
Overview of the Book

Welcome to the flavorful world of burgers, where every bite tells a story. In "Burgeropolis: A Culinary Expedition Through the World of Burgers," we embark on a mouthwatering journey to explore the history, culture, and evolution of one of the world's most beloved foods.

This book is a comprehensive exploration of the burger phenomenon, from its humble beginnings to its global dominance. Through meticulous research, engaging storytelling, and vibrant imagery, we dive deep into the origins, cultural significance, and culinary innovations that have shaped the burger into the iconic dish it is today.

Throughout the pages of "Burgeropolis," readers will discover the fascinating story of how the burger emerged from simple meat dishes to become a symbol of American identity and a culinary phenomenon embraced around the world. We'll trace its evolution from the earliest predecessors to the modern burger, exploring the influence of immigrant communities, the rise of fast-food chains, and the emergence of gourmet burger joints.

But "Burgeropolis" is more than just a history book; it's a celebration of the diverse flavors and traditions that make the burger a global culinary icon. From classic American diners to exotic burger creations from around the world, we'll take readers on a tantalizing tour of iconic burger joints, regional favorites, and celebrity chef-owned establishments.

In addition to exploring the cultural impact of the burger, "Burgeropolis" also delves into the culinary techniques and innovations that have revolutionized burger-making. Readers will learn the secrets behind choosing the perfect meat and ingredients, mastering grilling techniques, and creating signature sauces and toppings that elevate the humble burger into a gourmet masterpiece.

But our exploration doesn't stop there. We'll also examine the social, economic, and environmental impact of the burger industry, discussing topics such as urban development, job creation, sustainability, and ethical considerations surrounding meat consumption. And as we look to the future, we'll speculate on the technological innovations, changing consumer preferences, and emerging trends that will shape the future of burger culture.

With its rich storytelling, insightful analysis, and mouthwatering recipes, "Burgeropolis" offers something for everyone, from food enthusiasts and history buffs to culinary adventurers seeking to uncover the secrets of the world's favorite sandwich. So grab a bun, fire up the grill, and join us on a culinary expedition through the world of burgers.

Prepare to be inspired, tantalized, and utterly satisfied as we embark on this delicious journey together. Welcome to "Burgeropolis."

Why Burgers?

Why burgers? What is it about this humble sandwich that has captured the hearts, minds, and taste buds of people around the world? In this section, we delve into the significance and relevance of the burger, exploring why it holds such a special place in culinary history and contemporary culture.

At its core, the burger is more than just a meal; it's a symbol of comfort, familiarity, and community. For many, biting into a juicy burger evokes memories of backyard barbecues, family gatherings, and lazy summer days. It's a food that brings people together, transcending cultural boundaries and social divides.

But the appeal of the burger goes beyond nostalgia. In a world where culinary trends come and go, the burger remains a steadfast favorite, cherished by people of all ages and backgrounds. Its universal appeal lies in its simplicity and versatility; whether you prefer yours piled high with toppings or stripped down to the basics, there's a burger for everyone.

One of the reasons burgers hold such enduring popularity is their adaptability. From street food stalls to high-end restaurants, burgers can be found on menus around the world, each with its own unique twist. Whether it's a classic cheeseburger, a gourmet creation featuring exotic ingredients, or a plant-based alternative, the burger has the remarkable ability to evolve with the times while retaining its essence.

But perhaps the most compelling reason for the burger's continued relevance is its ability to reflect the cultural zeitgeist. As society changes, so too does the burger, mirroring shifting attitudes towards food, health, and sustainability. From the rise of fast-food chains in the post-war era to the current trend towards plant-based alternatives, the burger has always been a barometer of our culinary landscape.

In today's fast-paced world, where time is precious and convenience is king, the burger offers a quick, satisfying meal that doesn't skimp on flavor. Whether you're grabbing a burger on your lunch break or indulging in a late-night snack, it's a reliable choice that never disappoints.

But perhaps above all else, the enduring appeal of the burger lies in its ability to evoke joy. There's something undeniably joyful about sinking your teeth into a perfectly grilled patty, the juices running down your chin as you savor each bite. It's a simple pleasure that brings a smile to your face and a warmth to your heart.

In "Burgeropolis," we celebrate this joyous spirit of the burger, exploring its rich history, cultural significance, and culinary innovations. Join us as we embark on a culinary expedition through the world of burgers, from classic creations to cutting-edge cuisine. Prepare to be inspired, tantalized, and utterly satisfied as we explore the delicious world of burgers together.

Approach and Methodology

In crafting "Burgeropolis: A Culinary Expedition Through the World of Burgers," our approach and methodology are integral to ensuring a comprehensive and engaging exploration of the topic. In this section, we outline our approach to researching and presenting the history, culture, and evolution of burgers, as well as the methodologies employed to ensure accuracy, depth, and relevance.

Our approach to "Burgeropolis" is rooted in a commitment to thorough research, meticulous fact-checking, and a dedication to presenting a balanced and nuanced perspective on the subject matter. We understand the importance of treating burger culture with the respect and attention it deserves, acknowledging its significance as both a culinary phenomenon and a cultural touchstone.

To begin our exploration, we conducted extensive research into the history of burgers, tracing their origins from early meat dishes to their evolution into the modern sandwich we know today. This involved delving into historical records, culinary texts, and academic literature to uncover the key milestones, influences, and innovations that have shaped burger culture over the centuries.

In addition to historical research, we also sought to capture the contemporary landscape of burger culture, exploring current trends, innovations, and debates surrounding the dish. This involved engaging with experts in the field, conducting interviews with chefs, food historians, and industry insiders, and immersing ourselves in the world of burger-making through hands-on experiences and tastings.

Central to our methodology is a commitment to presenting a diverse range of perspectives and voices throughout the book. We recognize that burger culture is multifaceted and ever-evolving, shaped by a myriad of factors including geography, culture, and personal taste. As such, we have sought to incorporate a variety of viewpoints and experiences into our exploration, ensuring a rich and multifaceted portrayal of burger culture worldwide.

In presenting our findings, we have endeavored to strike a balance between informative content and engaging storytelling. While "Burgeropolis" is grounded in rigorous research and factual accuracy, we have also sought to bring the subject matter to life through vivid descriptions, anecdotes, and profiles of key figures in burger history.

Throughout the writing process, we have remained mindful of our audience, striving to make the content accessible and engaging to readers of all backgrounds and interests. Whether you're a seasoned food enthusiast or simply curious about the history and culture of burgers, we hope that "Burgeropolis" will offer something of interest and value to you.

In summary, "Burgeropolis" is the result of months of research, exploration, and passion for the subject matter. Through our approach and methodology, we have endeavored to present a comprehensive and engaging exploration of the world of burgers, celebrating their history, culture, and enduring appeal.

Chapter 1: Origins and Evolution
Predecessors to the Burger (Early meat dishes)

In order to understand the origins of the burger, it's essential to explore the predecessors to this iconic dish. The journey of the burger begins long before the modern sandwich we know today, with early meat dishes that laid the foundation for its creation.

Ancient civilizations around the world have a rich history of incorporating meat into their diets, often in the form of simple grilled or roasted preparations. While these early meat dishes may not resemble the burgers we're familiar with, they provide important insights into the evolution of our culinary traditions.

One of the earliest examples of a meat-based dish is the kebab, which traces its origins back to ancient Persia. The concept of skewering and grilling meat over an open flame has been practiced for thousands of years, with variations found in cultures across the Middle East, Central Asia, and the Mediterranean region. While kebabs typically consist of chunks of meat rather than ground meat patties, they share a similar principle of cooking meat over fire.

In ancient Rome, the concept of minced meat dishes was prevalent, with recipes for dishes such as isicia omentata, a type of spiced meatball made from minced meat mixed with bread crumbs, herbs, and spices. While these early meatballs were typically served without bread, they represent an early form of ground meat preparation that would later evolve into the burger.

In medieval Europe, minced meat dishes continued to be popular, with recipes for minced pies and patties appearing in cookbooks of the time. These dishes often featured a mixture of minced meat, spices, and other ingredients encased in pastry or served as savory pies. While these early meat pies may not resemble the burgers we're familiar with today, they demonstrate a continued interest in ground meat preparations.

The concept of grinding meat to create a uniform texture and shape gained popularity in the 18th and 19th centuries, particularly in Europe. In Germany, the city of Hamburg was renowned for its minced beef dishes, which were often served raw or lightly cooked. These dishes, known as "Hamburg steak" or "Hamburg-style beef," consisted of seasoned minced beef formed into patties and pan-fried or grilled.

It was from this tradition of minced meat dishes that the modern burger emerged. In the late 19th century, German immigrants brought their culinary traditions with them to the United States, where they began selling Hamburg-style beef patties from food carts and stalls. These early burgers were often served on a plate without bread, but the concept of a ground meat patty remained the same.

The evolution of the burger truly took off with the invention of the hamburger bun. In the early 20th century, entrepreneurs such as Oscar Weber Bilby and Louis Lassen began serving Hamburg-style beef patties between two slices of bread, making them easier to eat on the go. This innovation transformed the burger from a simple meat patty into a portable, handheld meal that would soon capture the hearts and stomachs of people around the world.

In summary, while the modern burger may seem like a distinctly American creation, its roots can be traced back to early meat dishes from cultures around the world. From ancient kebabs to medieval meat pies, the predecessors to the burger laid the foundation for its evolution into the beloved dish we know and love today.

Emergence of the Modern Burger (Development in the United States)

The emergence of the modern burger as we know it today is intricately tied to the history of the United States. While the concept of ground meat patties has roots in European culinary traditions, it was in America that the burger truly came into its own, evolving from a humble street food into a cultural icon.

The story of the modern burger begins in the late 19th century, in the bustling cities of the United States. During this time, urbanization was on the rise, and people were increasingly seeking out quick and convenient meals that could be enjoyed on the go. It was in this context that the Hamburg-style beef patty made its debut on the streets of American cities.

German immigrants, who had brought their culinary traditions with them to the United States, began selling Hamburg-style beef patties from food carts and stalls. These early burgers were simple affairs, consisting of seasoned minced beef formed into patties and cooked on a griddle. They were typically served without bread, often accompanied by onions, pickles, and condiments.

One of the earliest recorded instances of the term "hamburger" being used to describe the sandwich dates back to the late 19th century. In 1885, a reporter for the "Wallace's Farmer" newspaper in Iowa wrote about a "hamburger sandwich" being served at a county fair in Hamburg, New York. While the exact origins of the term are still debated, it's clear that the hamburger had begun to make a name for itself in American culinary culture.

The true turning point for the burger came with the invention of the hamburger bun. In the early 20th century, entrepreneurs such as Oscar Weber Bilby and Louis Lassen began serving Hamburg-style beef patties between two slices of bread, making them easier to eat on the go. This innovation transformed the burger from a simple meat patty into a portable, handheld meal that would soon capture the hearts and stomachs of people around the country.

The popularity of the burger skyrocketed in the early 20th century, thanks in part to the rise of fast-food chains and diners. Chains such as White Castle, founded in 1921 in Wichita, Kansas, and McDonald's, founded in 1940 in San Bernardino, California, helped to popularize the burger as a quick, affordable meal option for the masses. These chains standardized the burger-making process, introducing assembly-line techniques and uniformity in preparation and presentation.

The post-World War II era saw the burger cement its status as an iconic American food. The economic boom of the 1950s led to the proliferation of diners, drive-ins, and burger joints across the country, each serving up their own unique take on the classic sandwich. The burger became synonymous with American culture, representing the ideals of freedom, opportunity, and prosperity.

Throughout the latter half of the 20th century and into the 21st century, the burger continued to evolve and adapt to changing tastes and trends. Gourmet burger joints emerged, offering upscale interpretations of the classic sandwich with gourmet toppings and artisanal ingredients. Meanwhile, the rise of health-conscious eating led to the development of leaner, healthier burger options, including turkey, chicken, and plant-based alternatives.

Today, the burger remains as popular as ever, with countless variations and interpretations found on menus around the world. From classic cheeseburgers to exotic creations featuring unique ingredients and flavor combinations, the burger continues to captivate diners and inspire chefs with its endless possibilities.

In summary, the emergence of the modern burger in the United States is a testament to the country's rich culinary history and cultural diversity. From its humble beginnings as a street food to its status as a global culinary icon, the burger has left an indelible mark on American culture and cuisine, shaping the way we eat and enjoy food for generations to come.

Evolution of Ingredients and Toppings

The evolution of ingredients and toppings in the world of burgers is a fascinating journey that reflects changing tastes, culinary innovations, and cultural influences. From humble beginnings to gourmet creations, the burger has undergone a remarkable transformation in terms of the ingredients used to create it and the toppings added to enhance its flavor. In this section, we'll explore the evolution of ingredients and toppings in the burger, tracing their history from simple beginnings to the diverse array of options available today.

The earliest burgers were simple affairs, consisting of seasoned ground beef patties cooked on a griddle and served between two slices of bread. The ingredients used in these early burgers were straightforward and practical, reflecting the limited availability of ingredients and the need for quick, affordable meals.

One of the key ingredients in early burgers was beef, which was readily available and relatively inexpensive. Ground beef was seasoned with salt, pepper, and other spices to enhance its flavor, and formed into patties before being cooked on a griddle. The result was a simple yet satisfying meal that appealed to a wide range of tastes.

As the popularity of burgers grew, so too did the variety of ingredients used to create them. In addition to beef, other types of meat such as pork, chicken, and turkey began to be used in burgers, offering a lighter and leaner alternative to traditional beef burgers. These alternative meat options provided greater variety and catered to the diverse tastes and dietary preferences of consumers.

In addition to meat, a variety of other ingredients began to be added to burgers to enhance their flavor and texture. Cheese, for example, became a popular topping for burgers, adding richness and creaminess to the dish. While early burgers were typically served without cheese, the addition of cheese soon became a standard feature of many burger recipes, giving rise to the classic cheeseburger.

The evolution of toppings in the burger is perhaps one of the most significant developments in its history. While early burgers were often served with simple toppings such as onions, pickles, and condiments, the range of toppings available today is virtually limitless. From classic toppings like lettuce, tomato, and onion to more adventurous options like avocado, bacon, and fried eggs, the variety of toppings available allows for endless customization and creativity in burger-making.

The evolution of ingredients and toppings in the burger has also been influenced by cultural factors and regional preferences. In different parts of the world, burgers are made with a wide range of ingredients and toppings that reflect local culinary traditions and tastes. For example, in the United States, classic toppings like ketchup, mustard, and mayonnaise are commonly used, while in Mexico, burgers may be topped with ingredients like guacamole, salsa, and jalapenos.

In recent years, there has been a growing emphasis on using high-quality, locally-sourced ingredients in burger-making. Chefs and restaurateurs are increasingly focused on creating burgers that not only taste delicious but also showcase the flavors and ingredients of the regions in which they are made. This trend towards gourmet burger-making has led to the emergence of specialty burger joints and restaurants that offer unique and innovative takes on the classic sandwich.

Overall, the evolution of ingredients and toppings in the burger is a testament to the versatility and adaptability of this beloved dish. From its humble beginnings as a simple meat patty between two slices of bread to the gourmet creations available today, the burger continues to evolve and inspire with its endless possibilities.

Influence of Immigrant Communities

The influence of immigrant communities on the origins and evolution of the burger is a fascinating aspect of its history. Throughout the years, various immigrant groups have brought their culinary traditions, flavors, and techniques to the United States, contributing to the rich tapestry of American cuisine. In this section, we'll explore how immigrant communities have influenced the development of the burger, shaping its ingredients, flavors, and cultural significance.

One of the earliest influences on the burger came from German immigrants who arrived in the United States in the 19th century. These immigrants brought with them a tradition of minced meat dishes, including Hamburg-style beef patties, which laid the foundation for the modern burger. Hamburg-style beef patties, made from seasoned minced beef formed into patties and cooked on a griddle, were popular among German immigrants and soon gained popularity among Americans of all backgrounds.

In addition to Hamburg-style beef patties, German immigrants also introduced other culinary traditions that would influence the development of the burger. Sauerkraut, for example, became a popular topping for burgers, adding tanginess and texture to the dish. Meanwhile, the concept of serving meat between two slices of bread, rather than on a plate, was also a German innovation that helped to popularize the burger as a handheld meal.

Italian immigrants also played a significant role in shaping the burger's evolution in the United States. Italian-

American cuisine, with its emphasis on bold flavors and hearty ingredients, had a profound influence on American culinary culture, including the burger. Italian immigrants introduced ingredients such as garlic, oregano, and Parmesan cheese to the American palate, which were often used to flavor burgers and meatballs.

One of the most iconic Italian-inspired burgers is the pizza burger, which combines the flavors of a traditional pizza with the convenience of a burger. Typically made with a beef patty seasoned with Italian spices, topped with marinara sauce, mozzarella cheese, and pepperoni, the pizza burger is a delicious fusion of two beloved comfort foods.

In addition to German and Italian immigrants, other immigrant communities have also left their mark on the burger's evolution. Jewish immigrants, for example, introduced ingredients such as kosher pickles and pastrami, which became popular toppings for burgers. Meanwhile, Greek immigrants brought their tradition of grilling meats and serving them with tzatziki sauce and feta cheese, influencing the development of the Greek-inspired burger.

In recent years, the influence of immigrant communities on the burger has only grown stronger as America's culinary landscape becomes increasingly diverse. Asian-inspired burgers, for example, have become increasingly popular, with toppings such as teriyaki sauce, kimchi, and sriracha adding a unique twist to the classic sandwich. Meanwhile, Middle Eastern-inspired burgers, featuring ingredients such as falafel, tahini sauce, and hummus, offer a flavorful alternative to traditional beef burgers.

Overall, the influence of immigrant communities on the origins and evolution of the burger is a testament to the richness and diversity of American cuisine. Through their culinary traditions, flavors, and techniques, immigrant communities have helped to shape the burger into the beloved comfort food it is today, reflecting the melting pot of cultures that defines American society.

Chapter 2: Cultural Impact
Burger as a Symbol of American Identity

The burger holds a special place in American culture, serving as a symbol of American identity and embodying the values and ideals that define the nation. From its humble beginnings as a street food to its status as a global culinary icon, the burger has played a central role in shaping American culinary traditions and cultural identity.

One of the key factors contributing to the burger's status as a symbol of American identity is its association with the American Dream. The burger is often seen as a quintessentially American food, representing the ideals of freedom, opportunity, and prosperity. Its humble origins as a simple street food have made it accessible to people of all backgrounds and socioeconomic status, embodying the belief that anyone can achieve success and prosperity in America.

In addition to its association with the American Dream, the burger also embodies the spirit of innovation and entrepreneurship that is characteristic of American culture. Throughout its history, the burger has been a vehicle for culinary experimentation and innovation, with chefs and restaurateurs constantly pushing the boundaries of what is possible with this iconic dish. From gourmet creations featuring exotic ingredients to fast-food chains offering affordable and convenient options, the burger reflects the spirit of creativity and innovation that defines American cuisine.

The burger's status as a symbol of American identity is further reinforced by its widespread popularity and ubiquity in

American society. Burgers can be found on menus across the country, from roadside diners to high-end restaurants, catering to a diverse range of tastes and preferences. Its versatility and adaptability have made it a favorite among people of all ages and backgrounds, transcending cultural and regional divides to become a unifying symbol of American culture.

Furthermore, the burger's association with American popular culture has helped to solidify its status as a symbol of American identity. From iconic scenes in movies and television shows to memorable advertising campaigns and product placements, the burger has become deeply ingrained in the fabric of American popular culture. Its presence in popular media serves as a constant reminder of its status as a beloved and iconic American food.

The burger's role as a symbol of American identity extends beyond its culinary significance to encompass broader social and cultural themes. For many Americans, the burger represents more than just a meal; it is a symbol of shared experiences, traditions, and values that unite people across generations and backgrounds. Whether enjoyed at a backyard barbecue, a family picnic, or a roadside diner, the burger serves as a reminder of the simple pleasures of American life.

In conclusion, the burger's status as a symbol of American identity is rooted in its association with the American Dream, its spirit of innovation and entrepreneurship, its widespread popularity and ubiquity in American society, and its presence in American popular culture. As a beloved and iconic American food, the burger embodies the values, traditions, and ideals that define the nation, making it a fitting symbol of American identity.

Globalization and International Adaptations

The globalization of the burger is a testament to its universal appeal and adaptability. While the burger may have originated in the United States, it has since spread to every corner of the globe, becoming a beloved culinary staple in countries around the world. In this section, we'll explore the impact of globalization on the burger and the various international adaptations that have emerged as a result.

One of the key drivers of the globalization of the burger is the spread of American culture and influence around the world. As American brands and franchises expanded into international markets, they brought with them the iconic American burger, introducing people from diverse cultural backgrounds to this quintessential American food. Fast-food chains such as McDonald's, Burger King, and KFC played a central role in popularizing the burger on a global scale, offering a taste of American culture to consumers around the world.

However, while American fast-food chains may have introduced the burger to international audiences, the way it is consumed and enjoyed varies significantly from country to country. In many cases, international adaptations of the burger incorporate local ingredients, flavors, and culinary traditions, giving rise to unique and distinctive variations of the classic sandwich.

One example of a popular international adaptation of the burger is the ramen burger, which originated in Japan and has since gained popularity in other parts of the world. Instead of a traditional bun, the ramen burger features two patties made from cooked ramen noodles, which are then grilled and served with a variety of toppings and condiments. The result is a fusion of Japanese and American culinary traditions that offers a unique and flavorful twist on the classic burger.

In Australia, the "Aussie burger" is a popular variation that incorporates ingredients such as beetroot, pineapple, and fried egg, giving it a distinctively Australian flavor profile. Similarly, in South Korea, the "bulgogi burger" features marinated beef patties grilled and served with traditional Korean barbecue sauce, kimchi, and other Korean-inspired toppings.

In India, where beef consumption is limited due to cultural and religious beliefs, vegetarian burgers made from ingredients such as potatoes, peas, and lentils are a popular alternative. These vegetarian burgers are often spiced with Indian flavors such as cumin, coriander, and turmeric, giving them a unique and flavorful taste that appeals to Indian palates.

In addition to regional variations, the globalization of the burger has also led to the emergence of gourmet burger joints and upscale burger bars in cities around the world. These establishments offer a more refined and upscale take on the classic burger, using high-quality ingredients and innovative flavor combinations to create gourmet burgers that rival those found in fine dining restaurants.

Overall, the globalization of the burger has transformed it from a humble American street food into a global culinary phenomenon. From regional variations that incorporate local ingredients and flavors to gourmet creations that push the boundaries of traditional burger-making, the burger continues to evolve and adapt to the diverse tastes and preferences of consumers around the world.

Rituals and Traditions Surrounding Burger Consumption

Rituals and traditions surrounding burger consumption are deeply ingrained in cultures around the world, reflecting the significance of this iconic dish in people's lives. From backyard barbecues to fast-food outings, the act of enjoying a burger is often accompanied by a set of customs and rituals that enhance the experience and bring people together. In this section, we'll explore some of the common rituals and traditions surrounding burger consumption and their cultural significance.

One of the most enduring traditions associated with burger consumption is the backyard barbecue. In many parts of the world, especially in the United States, the burger is synonymous with outdoor grilling and social gatherings. Whether it's a Fourth of July cookout or a weekend barbecue with friends and family, firing up the grill and cooking burgers outdoors is a time-honored tradition that brings people together and fosters a sense of community.

The ritual of grilling burgers on the barbecue is often accompanied by other customs and traditions, such as the selection of condiments and toppings. From classic options like ketchup, mustard, and pickles to more adventurous choices like barbecue sauce, guacamole, and sriracha, the array of toppings available allows for endless customization and personalization, catering to the diverse tastes and preferences of grillmasters and guests alike.

Another common tradition associated with burger consumption is the act of ordering burgers at a fast-food restaurant. Fast-food chains such as McDonald's, Burger King, and Wendy's have become synonymous with the burger in many parts of the world, offering convenient and affordable options for people on the go. The ritual of ordering a burger at a fast-food restaurant often involves a set of familiar steps, from choosing the desired toppings and condiments to selecting sides and beverages to accompany the meal.

In addition to backyard barbecues and fast-food outings, the burger is also a popular choice for casual dining at restaurants and diners. Many restaurants offer a variety of burger options on their menus, ranging from classic cheeseburgers to gourmet creations featuring premium ingredients and artisanal toppings. The ritual of dining out for burgers often involves the anticipation of enjoying a delicious meal in a relaxed and comfortable setting, surrounded by friends, family, or fellow burger enthusiasts.

In some cultures, the act of eating burgers is associated with specific rituals and customs that have been passed down through generations. For example, in Japan, where the burger has gained popularity in recent years, there is a tradition of meticulously assembling and garnishing burgers with precision and care. This attention to detail reflects the Japanese concept of "omotenashi," or hospitality, and adds an element of ceremony to the act of enjoying a burger.

In summary, rituals and traditions surrounding burger consumption are an integral part of cultures around the world, reflecting the significance of this iconic dish in people's lives. Whether it's grilling burgers at a backyard barbecue, ordering burgers at a fast-food restaurant, or dining out for burgers at a restaurant or diner, the act of enjoying a burger is often accompanied by a set of customs and rituals that enhance the experience and bring people together.

Representation in Media and Pop Culture

The burger's representation in media and pop culture is a testament to its status as an iconic and beloved food item. From movies and television shows to advertising campaigns and product placements, the burger has become deeply ingrained in the fabric of popular culture, serving as a symbol of American life and values. In this section, we'll explore the various ways in which the burger is represented in media and pop culture and its significance in shaping cultural narratives and identities.

One of the most prominent ways in which the burger is represented in media and pop culture is through its portrayal in movies and television shows. Countless films and TV series feature scenes set in diners, fast-food restaurants, and burger joints, where characters are often seen enjoying burgers as a quick and satisfying meal. These scenes serve not only to advance the plot but also to evoke a sense of nostalgia and familiarity, as burgers are a ubiquitous and universally loved food item.

In addition to its portrayal in scripted entertainment, the burger is also featured prominently in reality TV shows and cooking competitions. Shows like "Diners, Drive-Ins and Dives" and "Man v. Food" often showcase unique and innovative burger creations from around the country, highlighting the creativity and diversity of burger culture in America. These shows not only celebrate the burger as a culinary icon but also offer insight into the people and places behind the food, fostering a deeper appreciation for the dish and its cultural significance.

Advertising is another key arena in which the burger is represented in pop culture. Fast-food chains such as McDonald's, Burger King, and Wendy's have launched countless advertising campaigns featuring burgers as the star attraction. These campaigns often employ catchy slogans, memorable jingles, and mouth-watering visuals to entice consumers and promote the appeal of their burger offerings. In many cases, burgers are portrayed as indulgent, crave-worthy treats that offer a taste of comfort and satisfaction.

Product placements in movies, TV shows, and music videos are another common way in which the burger is featured in pop culture. Whether it's a character enjoying a burger at a fast-food restaurant or a celebrity endorsing a burger brand in a commercial, these placements serve to reinforce the burger's status as a desirable and iconic food item. By associating burgers with popular and influential figures, brands are able to leverage the power of celebrity endorsement to enhance the appeal of their products and reach a wider audience.

The burger's representation in media and pop culture extends beyond traditional forms of entertainment to encompass a wide range of artistic mediums. Artists, photographers, and graphic designers often use burgers as subject matter in their work, creating visually striking images and installations that explore themes of consumerism, identity, and cultural symbolism. These artistic representations offer new perspectives on the burger as both a culinary object and a cultural artifact, challenging viewers to reconsider their assumptions and perceptions of the dish.

In summary, the burger's representation in media and pop culture is a reflection of its status as an iconic and beloved food item. From its portrayal in movies and television shows to its prominence in advertising campaigns and product placements, the burger serves as a symbol of American life and values, shaping cultural narratives and identities in profound and meaningful ways.

Chapter 3: Innovation and Trends
Invention of the Hamburger Bun

The invention of the hamburger bun marks a significant milestone in the evolution of the burger, transforming it from a simple meat patty between two slices of bread into the iconic sandwich we know and love today. The introduction of the hamburger bun revolutionized the way burgers were made, consumed, and enjoyed, paving the way for the widespread popularity of this beloved dish. In this section, we'll explore the history of the hamburger bun, its impact on burger culture, and its enduring legacy in the world of culinary innovation.

The origins of the hamburger bun can be traced back to the late 19th century, when the burger began to gain popularity as a street food in cities across the United States. At that time, burgers were typically served on a plate without bread, often accompanied by onions, pickles, and condiments. However, as the demand for burgers grew, so too did the need for a more convenient and portable way to enjoy them.

The invention of the hamburger bun is often credited to Oscar Weber Bilby, a cook at a cafe in Tulsa, Oklahoma, who reportedly came up with the idea in 1891. Bilby, who was looking for a way to make burgers easier to eat on the go, began serving them between two slices of bread, effectively creating the first prototype of the modern hamburger bun. This innovation made burgers more portable and easier to handle, paving the way for their widespread popularity as a fast and convenient meal option.

While Bilby may have been the first to serve burgers on buns, the concept of the hamburger bun quickly caught on and spread to other parts of the country. By the early 20th century, burger joints and diners across the United States were serving burgers on soft, squishy buns, a practice that soon became the standard for burger preparation.

The introduction of the hamburger bun revolutionized the burger-making process, making it easier and more efficient to assemble and serve burgers in large quantities. Instead of having to slice bread for each individual burger, cooks could simply place a patty between two pre-sliced buns, saving time and labor in the kitchen. This allowed burger joints and fast-food chains to serve burgers more quickly and efficiently, catering to the growing demand for this popular dish.

In addition to its practical advantages, the hamburger bun also had a significant impact on the way burgers were consumed and enjoyed. The soft, squishy texture of the bun provided a satisfying contrast to the juicy meat patty, creating a harmonious balance of flavors and textures that made burgers even more irresistible. The bun also helped to hold the burger together, preventing the filling from spilling out and making it easier to eat with your hands.

The invention of the hamburger bun also played a role in shaping the cultural significance of the burger. As burgers became more closely associated with buns, they came to symbolize not only a delicious and satisfying meal but also a quintessentially American food experience. The burger and bun combo became a staple of American cuisine, representing the ideals of convenience, innovation, and abundance that are central to American culture.

Over the years, the hamburger bun has undergone various iterations and improvements, with bakers experimenting with different shapes, sizes, and textures to suit the evolving tastes and preferences of consumers. Today, hamburger buns come in a wide range of varieties, from traditional sesame seed buns to gourmet options made with artisanal ingredients such as brioche or pretzel dough. These specialty buns add an extra layer of flavor and sophistication to burgers, elevating them from a simple street food to a gourmet culinary delight.

In conclusion, the invention of the hamburger bun was a transformative moment in the history of the burger, revolutionizing the way it was made, consumed, and enjoyed. From its humble beginnings in a small cafe in Oklahoma to its widespread popularity as a staple of American cuisine, the hamburger bun has left an indelible mark on burger culture, shaping the way we eat and enjoy this beloved dish for generations to come.

Rise of Fast-Food Chains

The rise of fast-food chains has had a profound impact on the burger industry, shaping the way burgers are made, consumed, and perceived around the world. From humble beginnings as small roadside stands to global empires with thousands of locations, fast-food chains have played a central role in popularizing the burger as a convenient and affordable meal option for millions of people. In this section, we'll explore the history of fast-food chains and their influence on burger culture, innovation, and trends.

The origins of the fast-food industry can be traced back to the early 20th century, when entrepreneurs such as White Castle founder Billy Ingram and McDonald's founders Richard and Maurice McDonald began selling hamburgers and other quick-service meals from small roadside stands and drive-ins. These early pioneers of the fast-food industry recognized the growing demand for convenient and affordable meal options, particularly among urban dwellers and travelers, and sought to capitalize on this emerging market.

One of the key innovations introduced by fast-food chains was the concept of assembly-line cooking, which allowed for the mass production of burgers and other menu items in a quick and efficient manner. By standardizing the cooking process and streamlining operations, fast-food chains were able to serve large volumes of customers with minimal wait times, making it possible to order and receive a burger in a matter of minutes.

Another important innovation introduced by fast-food chains was the concept of franchising, which allowed for rapid expansion and growth. Franchising enabled fast-food chains to open new locations in cities and towns across the country, often with relatively low overhead costs and minimal risk to the parent company. This allowed fast-food chains to quickly establish a presence in new markets and reach a wider audience, further fueling their growth and success.

The post-World War II era saw a boom in the fast-food industry, with new chains and concepts emerging to meet the growing demand for quick and convenient meal options. Chains such as Burger King, Taco Bell, and KFC capitalized on the popularity of burgers and other fast-food staples, offering a wide range of menu options to appeal to diverse tastes and preferences. These chains introduced innovations such as drive-thru windows, indoor seating, and value meals, further enhancing the convenience and accessibility of fast-food dining.

One of the most iconic and influential fast-food chains of all time is McDonald's, which was founded in 1940 by Richard and Maurice McDonald in San Bernardino, California. McDonald's pioneered many of the innovations that have come to define the fast-food industry, including the assembly-line cooking process, the drive-thru window, and the concept of franchising. With its iconic golden arches and famous menu items such as the Big Mac and Quarter Pounder, McDonald's quickly became synonymous with fast-food dining and helped to popularize the burger as a staple of American cuisine.

In addition to their impact on burger culture, fast-food chains have also played a significant role in shaping broader cultural trends and attitudes towards food and dining. The rise of fast-food chains has been accompanied by a shift towards convenience and efficiency in dining habits, with many people opting for quick-service meals over traditional sit-down dining experiences. This shift has had implications for the way people eat, socialize, and interact with food, contributing to the rise of on-the-go eating and the decline of traditional meal times and rituals.

Despite their popularity and influence, fast-food chains have also faced criticism and controversy over the years, particularly regarding issues such as nutrition, health, and labor practices. Critics argue that fast food is often high in calories, fat, and sodium, contributing to obesity, heart disease, and other health problems. Additionally, fast-food workers have raised concerns about low wages, poor working conditions, and limited opportunities for advancement within the industry.

In response to these criticisms, many fast-food chains have made efforts to improve the nutritional quality of their menu offerings and implement more sustainable and ethical business practices. This has led to the introduction of healthier menu options, such as salads, grilled chicken sandwiches, and fruit smoothies, as well as initiatives to source ingredients responsibly and reduce environmental impact.

Overall, the rise of fast-food chains has had a profound impact on the burger industry and broader culinary landscape, shaping the way burgers are made, consumed, and perceived around the world. While fast-food chains have faced criticism and controversy, they have also played a central role in popularizing the burger as a convenient and affordable meal option for millions of people, contributing to its status as a beloved and iconic food item.

Gourmet Burger Revolution

The gourmet burger revolution represents a significant evolution in the burger industry, transforming the humble fast-food staple into a gourmet culinary delight. Fueled by a growing demand for high-quality ingredients, innovative flavor combinations, and artisanal preparation methods, the gourmet burger movement has redefined the way we think about burgers and elevated them to the status of gourmet cuisine. In this section, we'll explore the history of the gourmet burger revolution, its key drivers and influences, and its lasting impact on burger culture and culinary trends.

The roots of the gourmet burger revolution can be traced back to the late 20th century, when chefs and restaurateurs began to experiment with new and innovative ways to elevate the humble burger into a gourmet culinary experience. Inspired by the farm-to-table movement and a growing interest in artisanal food production, these pioneers of the gourmet burger movement sought to reimagine the classic burger using high-quality, locally-sourced ingredients and artisanal preparation techniques.

One of the key drivers of the gourmet burger revolution was a growing demand for transparency and authenticity in food production. As consumers became more educated about the origins of their food and the impact of their dietary choices on health and the environment, they began to seek out alternatives to mass-produced, factory-farmed burgers. This shift in consumer preferences created a demand for burgers made with sustainable, ethically-sourced ingredients and prepared using traditional cooking methods.

Another important influence on the gourmet burger revolution was the rise of the foodie movement and the increasing popularity of food-focused media such as cooking shows, food blogs, and culinary magazines. As consumers became more adventurous in their dining habits and more knowledgeable about food and cooking techniques, they began to seek out unique and innovative dining experiences, including gourmet burgers made with premium ingredients and creative flavor combinations.

The gourmet burger revolution was also fueled by a growing interest in culinary experimentation and innovation among chefs and restaurateurs. With the rise of celebrity chefs and the proliferation of upscale dining establishments, burgers were no longer confined to fast-food joints and diners but began to appear on the menus of high-end restaurants and gastropubs. Chefs embraced the challenge of reimagining the classic burger using unconventional ingredients and techniques, resulting in a proliferation of gourmet burger creations that pushed the boundaries of traditional burger-making.

One of the defining characteristics of the gourmet burger revolution is the emphasis on high-quality ingredients and artisanal preparation methods. Gourmet burgers are typically made with premium cuts of meat, such as grass-fed beef, wagyu beef, or dry-aged beef, which are known for their superior flavor and texture. These premium meats are often ground in-house and formed into patties by hand, ensuring maximum freshness and quality.

In addition to high-quality meat, gourmet burgers often feature a variety of upscale toppings and condiments that add depth and complexity to the flavor profile. From artisanal cheeses and house-made sauces to gourmet pickles and locally-sourced produce, the toppings used in gourmet burgers are carefully selected to complement and enhance the natural flavor of the meat. Many gourmet burger joints also offer a selection of creative and innovative burger creations, featuring unique flavor combinations inspired by global culinary traditions.

The gourmet burger revolution has also led to a proliferation of specialty burger joints and upscale burger bars in cities around the world. These establishments offer a more refined and upscale dining experience, with stylish decor, attentive service, and an extensive selection of gourmet burgers and craft beers. Many gourmet burger joints also pride themselves on their commitment to sustainability and ethical sourcing, using locally-sourced ingredients and eco-friendly packaging whenever possible.

In recent years, the gourmet burger revolution has continued to evolve and expand, with chefs and restaurateurs pushing the boundaries of burger-making even further. From gourmet sliders and stuffed burgers to vegan and vegetarian options, the gourmet burger movement has expanded to include a wide range of innovative creations that cater to diverse tastes and dietary preferences. As consumers continue to demand high-quality, artisanal food experiences, the gourmet burger revolution shows no signs of slowing down, ensuring that the humble burger will remain a beloved and iconic dish for generations to come.

Sustainability and Ethical Considerations

Sustainability and ethical considerations have become increasingly important factors in the burger industry, as consumers and businesses alike seek to minimize their environmental impact and promote responsible sourcing practices. From reducing carbon emissions and conserving natural resources to ensuring fair labor practices and animal welfare standards, sustainability and ethics are shaping the way burgers are produced, consumed, and perceived around the world. In this section, we'll explore the various ways in which sustainability and ethical considerations are influencing the burger industry and driving innovation and change.

One of the key sustainability challenges facing the burger industry is the environmental impact of beef production. Beef production is resource-intensive and has been linked to deforestation, greenhouse gas emissions, and water pollution. As the demand for burgers continues to rise, so too does the need to address these environmental concerns and find ways to produce beef more sustainably.

One approach to addressing the environmental impact of beef production is to promote sustainable farming practices that minimize resource use and reduce environmental harm. This includes practices such as rotational grazing, which helps to restore soil health and reduce erosion, and regenerative agriculture, which sequesters carbon in the soil and enhances ecosystem resilience. By adopting these sustainable farming practices, beef producers can mitigate the environmental impact of beef production and promote the long-term health and sustainability of the land.

Another strategy for promoting sustainability in the burger industry is to reduce food waste and promote efficiency throughout the supply chain. Food waste is a major contributor to greenhouse gas emissions and other environmental problems, and reducing waste can help to minimize the environmental footprint of burger production. This includes efforts to optimize packaging and distribution processes, minimize spoilage and shrinkage, and divert food waste from landfills through composting and recycling.

In addition to addressing environmental concerns, the burger industry is also grappling with ethical considerations related to animal welfare and fair labor practices. As consumers become more conscious of where their food comes from and how it is produced, there is growing demand for burgers made with humanely-raised, ethically-sourced ingredients. This has led to increased scrutiny of factory farming practices and calls for greater transparency and accountability in the food industry.

One approach to promoting animal welfare in the burger industry is to source beef from producers that adhere to high animal welfare standards and humane slaughter practices. This includes sourcing beef from pasture-raised cattle that are allowed to graze on open pasture and live in natural, low-stress environments. By prioritizing animal welfare in beef production, burger producers can ensure that their products are produced in a responsible and ethical manner.

In addition to animal welfare considerations, the burger industry is also facing pressure to address issues related to fair labor practices and worker rights. This includes ensuring fair wages and working conditions for farmworkers, slaughterhouse employees, and other workers throughout the burger supply chain. By promoting fair labor practices and supporting initiatives to improve working conditions, burger producers can help to ensure that their products are produced ethically and sustainably.

Many burger producers and fast-food chains have already taken steps to address sustainability and ethical considerations in their operations. This includes initiatives to reduce greenhouse gas emissions, conserve water and energy, and promote responsible sourcing practices. Some companies have also introduced plant-based burger options as a more sustainable and ethical alternative to traditional beef burgers.

Overall, sustainability and ethical considerations are shaping the way burgers are produced, consumed, and perceived in today's world. By addressing environmental concerns, promoting animal welfare, and supporting fair labor practices, the burger industry can help to create a more sustainable and ethical food system that benefits both people and the planet.

Chapter 4: Iconic Burger Joints
Classic Diners and Drive-Ins

Classic diners and drive-ins hold a special place in the hearts of burger enthusiasts, serving as nostalgic reminders of a bygone era when burgers were simple, affordable, and delicious. These iconic establishments have been serving up burgers and other comfort foods for decades, providing a taste of Americana and a glimpse into the country's culinary history. In this section, we'll explore the history of classic diners and drive-ins, their enduring appeal, and their significance in burger culture.

The origins of classic diners can be traced back to the late 19th century, when horse-drawn lunch wagons began to appear in cities across the United States, offering quick and affordable meals to urban workers. These early diners were simple affairs, consisting of little more than a wagon outfitted with a griddle and a few stools for customers to sit on. However, they quickly gained popularity thanks to their convenient location, affordable prices, and hearty fare.

As the automobile became increasingly popular in the early 20th century, diners began to evolve to meet the needs of a new generation of customers on the go. Diners started to take on the familiar form of roadside eateries with a distinctive stainless steel exterior, neon signage, and a counter with swivel stools. These classic diners became popular gathering places for families, friends, and travelers, offering a welcoming atmosphere and a menu of classic comfort foods, including burgers, fries, milkshakes, and pies.

Drive-ins, or drive-in restaurants, emerged as a popular dining concept in the 1920s and 1930s, offering customers the convenience of ordering and eating from their cars. Drive-ins typically featured carhops, or waitstaff on roller skates, who would take orders and deliver food directly to customers' cars. This novel dining experience quickly caught on, especially among teenagers and young adults, who enjoyed the freedom and independence of dining out without leaving their cars.

One of the most iconic features of classic diners and drive-ins is their menu of classic comfort foods, including burgers. These establishments often serve up burgers made with fresh, never-frozen beef patties, grilled to perfection and served on a toasted bun with a variety of toppings and condiments. The burgers are typically accompanied by classic sides such as fries, onion rings, and coleslaw, as well as milkshakes, sodas, and other beverages.

Classic diners and drive-ins are also known for their nostalgic atmosphere and retro decor, which harkens back to a simpler time. Many diners feature vintage furnishings, jukeboxes, and neon signs, evoking a sense of nostalgia and Americana that resonates with customers of all ages. The cozy booths, chrome accents, and checkerboard floors create a welcoming and inviting ambiance that makes diners and drive-ins popular destinations for families, friends, and travelers alike.

In addition to their nostalgic charm, classic diners and drive-ins play an important role in preserving culinary traditions and regional flavors. Many diners specialize in regional favorites and specialty burgers that reflect the unique tastes and preferences of their local communities. Whether it's a chili cheeseburger in Texas, a patty melt in California, or a butter burger in Wisconsin, classic diners and drive-ins offer a taste of regional cuisine that can't be found anywhere else.

Despite their nostalgic appeal, classic diners and drive-ins have faced challenges in recent years, as changing demographics, rising operating costs, and increased competition from fast-food chains have threatened their viability. Many classic diners have been forced to close their doors or adapt to changing consumer preferences in order to survive. However, those that have managed to weather the storm continue to thrive, thanks to their loyal customer base and commitment to quality, service, and tradition.

In conclusion, classic diners and drive-ins are an integral part of burger culture, serving as nostalgic reminders of a simpler time when burgers were enjoyed with friends and family at roadside eateries. These iconic establishments have been serving up delicious burgers and other comfort foods for generations, providing a taste of Americana and a glimpse into the country's culinary history. While classic diners and drive-ins may face challenges in today's fast-paced world, their enduring appeal and timeless charm ensure that they will remain beloved destinations for burger lovers for years to come.

Regional Favorites and Specialty Burgers

Regional favorites and specialty burgers are an integral part of burger culture, offering a diverse array of flavors, ingredients, and culinary traditions that reflect the unique tastes and preferences of different regions and communities. From chili burgers in the Southwest to pimento cheeseburgers in the South, these regional favorites and specialty burgers celebrate the rich tapestry of American cuisine and showcase the creativity and ingenuity of local chefs and restaurateurs. In this section, we'll explore some of the most iconic regional favorites and specialty burgers from around the country, highlighting their distinctive flavors and cultural significance.

One of the most iconic regional favorites is the Juicy Lucy, a specialty burger that hails from Minneapolis, Minnesota. The Juicy Lucy is made by sandwiching a slice of cheese between two beef patties and sealing the edges together, creating a molten core of melted cheese that oozes out with every bite. This unique burger is a favorite among locals and visitors alike, who flock to Minneapolis to experience its gooey, cheesy goodness firsthand.

In the Southwest, chili burgers are a popular regional specialty, with variations found in states like Texas, New Mexico, and Arizona. These hearty burgers are typically topped with a generous serving of chili con carne, along with traditional garnishes such as shredded cheese, onions, and jalapenos. The combination of spicy chili and juicy beef makes for a bold and flavorful burger that satisfies even the heartiest appetites.

In the Pacific Northwest, the salmon burger is a popular regional specialty that showcases the region's abundance of fresh seafood. Made with wild-caught salmon seasoned with herbs and spices, these burgers are grilled to perfection and served on a toasted bun with lettuce, tomato, and a tangy dill sauce. The salmon burger offers a delicious alternative to traditional beef burgers and highlights the region's commitment to sustainable seafood practices.

In the South, pimento cheeseburgers are a beloved regional favorite that combines two iconic Southern ingredients: pimento cheese and burgers. Pimento cheese, a creamy spread made with cheddar cheese, mayonnaise, and diced pimentos, is slathered generously onto a grilled beef patty and served on a toasted bun with traditional Southern fixings such as lettuce, tomato, and pickles. The result is a rich and indulgent burger that celebrates the flavors of the South.

In the Midwest, the butter burger is a classic regional specialty that has been delighting burger lovers for generations. Originating in Wisconsin, the butter burger is made by topping a grilled beef patty with a generous slab of butter, which melts into the meat and creates a rich and flavorful sauce. The burger is then served on a toasted bun with traditional toppings such as onions, pickles, and mustard, resulting in a decadent and delicious culinary indulgence.

In California, the In-N-Out Burger is an iconic regional favorite that has achieved cult status among burger aficionados. Known for its simple yet delicious menu of burgers, fries, and shakes, In-N-Out Burger has been serving up quality fast food since 1948. The chain's signature burger, the Double-Double, features two beef patties, two slices of American cheese, lettuce, tomato, onion, and a special sauce, all served on a toasted bun. The In-N-Out Burger has become synonymous with California culture and is a must-visit destination for burger lovers visiting the Golden State.

In the Northeast, the lobster roll burger is a popular regional specialty that combines two New England classics: the lobster roll and the burger. Made with fresh lobster meat tossed in a creamy mayonnaise dressing and served on a buttery toasted bun, the lobster roll burger offers a delicious twist on the traditional burger and highlights the region's love of seafood.

In the Deep South, the crawfish burger is a unique regional specialty that showcases the flavors of Louisiana's famous Cajun cuisine. Made with seasoned crawfish meat and served on a toasted bun with lettuce, tomato, and remoulade sauce, the crawfish burger offers a taste of the Gulf Coast and is a favorite among locals and visitors alike.

In the Rocky Mountains, the bison burger is a popular regional specialty that celebrates the region's abundant wildlife and ranching heritage. Made with lean and flavorful bison meat, these burgers are grilled to perfection and served on a toasted bun with traditional toppings such as lettuce, tomato, and onion. The bison burger offers a healthier alternative to traditional beef burgers and highlights the region's commitment to sustainable and ethical food production.

Overall, regional favorites and specialty burgers offer a delicious and diverse array of flavors and culinary traditions that celebrate the rich tapestry of American cuisine. From Juicy Lucys in the Midwest to crawfish burgers in the Deep South, these iconic burgers showcase the creativity and ingenuity of local chefs and restaurateurs and highlight the unique flavors and ingredients of different regions and communities.

Celebrity Chef-Owned Establishments

Celebrity chef-owned establishments have become a prominent fixture in the burger industry, offering diners a unique and upscale dining experience that combines gourmet culinary expertise with the timeless appeal of the classic burger. These iconic burger joints, helmed by renowned chefs and culinary innovators, elevate the humble burger into a culinary masterpiece, showcasing innovative flavor combinations, premium ingredients, and expert craftsmanship. In this section, we'll explore the phenomenon of celebrity chef-owned burger joints, their impact on burger culture, and some notable examples of these esteemed establishments.

Celebrity chef-owned burger joints represent a convergence of two culinary worlds: the world of haute cuisine and the world of casual comfort food. These establishments combine the creativity and culinary expertise of acclaimed chefs with the accessibility and familiarity of the classic burger, resulting in a dining experience that is both elevated and approachable. Celebrity chefs bring their signature style, expertise, and attention to detail to the burger-making process, resulting in burgers that are anything but ordinary.

One of the key features of celebrity chef-owned burger joints is the emphasis on high-quality ingredients and artisanal preparation methods. Celebrity chefs are known for their commitment to sourcing the finest ingredients, often from local and sustainable sources, and this dedication to quality is reflected in the burgers they serve. From premium cuts of beef to house-made condiments and artisanal cheeses, every element of the burger is carefully curated and crafted to perfection.

In addition to high-quality ingredients, celebrity chef-owned burger joints often offer a wide range of creative and innovative flavor combinations that push the boundaries of traditional burger-making. These chefs are not afraid to experiment with unexpected ingredients and bold flavors, resulting in burgers that are as unique as they are delicious. From truffle-infused patties to foie gras toppings to exotic spice blends, celebrity chef-owned burger joints offer a culinary adventure for the taste buds.

Another distinguishing feature of celebrity chef-owned burger joints is the attention to detail and craftsmanship that goes into every aspect of the dining experience. From the design of the restaurant to the presentation of the food to the service provided to guests, every element is carefully considered and executed to create a memorable and immersive dining experience. Celebrity chefs bring their passion, creativity, and expertise to bear on every aspect of the restaurant, ensuring that every guest leaves satisfied and impressed.

One of the most notable examples of a celebrity chef-owned burger joint is Gordon Ramsay Burger, located in Las Vegas. Helmed by renowned chef Gordon Ramsay, this upscale burger joint offers a menu of gourmet burgers made with premium ingredients and expert craftsmanship. From the signature Hell's Kitchen Burger to the Truffle Burger to the Farm Burger, each burger is a culinary masterpiece that showcases Ramsay's trademark flair and expertise.

Another celebrity chef-owned burger joint that has garnered acclaim is Bobby's Burger Palace, founded by celebrity chef Bobby Flay. With locations across the United States, Bobby's Burger Palace offers a menu of inventive and flavorful burgers inspired by Flay's travels and culinary experiences. From the Crunchburger to the Santa Fe Burger to the Miami Burger, each burger is a celebration of bold flavors and creative combinations that reflect Flay's passion for global cuisine.

In addition to Gordon Ramsay Burger and Bobby's Burger Palace, there are many other celebrity chef-owned burger joints that have made a mark on the culinary world. From Shake Shack, founded by renowned restaurateur Danny Meyer, to Wahlburgers, founded by actor Mark Wahlberg and his family, these establishments offer a diverse range of gourmet burgers that cater to a variety of tastes and preferences.

Overall, celebrity chef-owned burger joints represent a fusion of culinary expertise, creativity, and accessibility that has transformed the humble burger into a gourmet dining experience. These esteemed establishments offer diners the opportunity to enjoy expertly crafted burgers made with the finest ingredients and innovative flavor combinations, all while basking in the ambiance of a celebrity chef's culinary vision. With their commitment to quality, creativity, and craftsmanship, celebrity chef-owned burger joints continue to push the boundaries of burger culture and redefine the dining experience for burger enthusiasts around the world.

Legacy and Longevity of Iconic Burger Joints

The legacy and longevity of iconic burger joints are testaments to their enduring appeal and cultural significance. These beloved establishments have stood the test of time, weathering economic downturns, changing consumer tastes, and fierce competition to become cherished landmarks in their communities and beyond. In this section, we'll explore the rich history and lasting impact of iconic burger joints, from their humble beginnings to their status as cultural institutions.

Iconic burger joints often have humble beginnings, starting as small mom-and-pop operations or roadside stands serving up simple yet satisfying burgers to hungry customers. These establishments are often family-owned and operated, with recipes passed down through generations and a commitment to quality and tradition that sets them apart from their competitors.

One of the key factors contributing to the longevity of iconic burger joints is their ability to adapt and evolve with the times while staying true to their roots. While many burger joints have come and gone over the years, the ones that endure are often those that embrace change while maintaining the core elements that made them successful in the first place. Whether it's updating the menu to reflect changing tastes, renovating the interior to attract new customers, or expanding into new markets to reach a wider audience, iconic burger joints are always looking for ways to stay relevant and competitive in an ever-changing industry.

Another factor contributing to the legacy and longevity of iconic burger joints is their strong ties to their local communities. These establishments often serve as gathering places for friends, families, and neighbors, providing a sense of belonging and camaraderie that is hard to find elsewhere. Whether it's sponsoring local sports teams, hosting community events, or supporting charitable causes, iconic burger joints play an active role in the fabric of their communities, forging strong bonds with their customers that can last a lifetime.

Many iconic burger joints also have a rich history and cultural significance that adds to their appeal and longevity. Whether it's a historic building with architectural significance, a famous owner or founder with a colorful backstory, or a connection to a significant event or milestone in local history, these establishments often have stories to tell that capture the imagination and intrigue of their patrons. These stories help to create a sense of nostalgia and nostalgia that keeps customers coming back year after year, generation after generation.

In addition to their history and cultural significance, the quality and consistency of the food served at iconic burger joints are also key factors in their longevity. These establishments often take pride in using high-quality ingredients and time-tested recipes to create burgers that are consistently delicious and satisfying. Whether it's the secret sauce, the perfectly seasoned patty, or the freshly baked bun, iconic burger joints know that the key to success lies in serving up food that keeps customers coming back for more.

One of the most iconic and enduring burger joints in the United States is In-N-Out Burger, founded in 1948 by Harry and Esther Snyder in Baldwin Park, California. Known for its simple yet delicious burgers, fresh ingredients, and cult-like following, In-N-Out Burger has become a beloved institution in California and beyond. Despite its modest beginnings, the chain has grown to become one of the most recognizable and successful burger chains in the country, with a fiercely loyal fan base and a commitment to quality that has remained unchanged over the years.

Another iconic burger joint with a storied history is Louis' Lunch, located in New Haven, Connecticut. Founded in 1895 by Louis Lassen, Louis' Lunch claims to be the birthplace of the hamburger sandwich, having served up its famous "steak sandwiches" for over a century. The restaurant, which is housed in a small brick building that dates back to the late 19th century, has become a pilgrimage site for burger enthusiasts from around the world, drawing visitors eager to taste a piece of burger history.

Other iconic burger joints with a legacy of longevity include The Apple Pan in Los Angeles, California, which has been serving up its famous hickory burgers and homemade pies since 1947, and White Manna in Hackensack, New Jersey, which has been flipping burgers on its iconic diner-style grill since 1946. These establishments, along with countless others like them, have become cherished landmarks in their communities, beloved by locals and visitors alike for their delicious food, friendly service, and timeless appeal.

In conclusion, the legacy and longevity of iconic burger joints are a testament to their enduring appeal and cultural significance. These beloved establishments have stood the test of time, weathering economic downturns, changing consumer tastes, and fierce competition to become cherished landmarks in their communities and beyond. Whether it's their humble beginnings, strong ties to their local communities, rich history and cultural significance, or commitment to quality and consistency, iconic burger joints continue to capture the hearts and appetites of burger enthusiasts around the world, ensuring that their legacy will endure for generations to come.

Chapter 5: Health and Nutrition
Perceptions of Burger Consumption Over Time

Perceptions of burger consumption have evolved significantly over time, reflecting changing attitudes towards diet, health, and food production. From its humble beginnings as a simple and affordable meal to its current status as a symbol of indulgence and excess, the burger has undergone a transformation in the public consciousness, with perceptions shaped by cultural, social, and economic factors. In this section, we'll explore the changing perceptions of burger consumption over time, from its early days as a staple of the working class diet to its current status as a contentious symbol of dietary excess and health concerns.

In the early 20th century, burgers were considered a convenient and affordable option for urban workers and immigrants looking for a quick and filling meal. Often sold from carts, stands, and diners, burgers were seen as a practical and economical choice for those on the go, offering a satisfying meal that could be eaten with one hand. However, burgers were also associated with lower-income neighborhoods and working-class culture, leading some to view them as cheap and unhealthy fare.

During World War II, burgers gained popularity as a patriotic food choice, with government officials encouraging Americans to consume them as a way to support the war effort. With meat rationing in effect and food shortages looming, burgers became a symbol of American resilience and ingenuity, with slogans like "Hamburgers: The Victory Sandwich" encouraging citizens to do their part for the war effort by enjoying a burger.

In the postwar era, burgers continued to rise in popularity, becoming a staple of the American diet and a symbol of prosperity and progress. With the advent of fast-food chains like McDonald's and Burger King in the 1950s and 1960s, burgers became more accessible than ever, with millions of Americans flocking to these new restaurants to enjoy their favorite fast-food fare. Burgers were no longer seen as a working-class meal but as a quintessentially American indulgence, synonymous with freedom, convenience, and modernity.

However, as the fast-food industry grew and burgers became more ubiquitous, concerns began to emerge about their nutritional content and health implications. With their high fat, sodium, and calorie content, burgers were increasingly viewed as a contributing factor to rising rates of obesity, heart disease, and other diet-related illnesses. Critics argued that the convenience and affordability of fast-food burgers came at a steep price, with public health experts warning of the dangers of excessive burger consumption.

Throughout the 1980s and 1990s, as concerns about diet and health continued to escalate, burgers came under increasing scrutiny from health advocates, government officials, and the media. Documentaries like "Super Size Me" and books like "Fast Food Nation" exposed the dark side of the fast-food industry, shining a spotlight on the health risks associated with frequent burger consumption and the environmental and ethical implications of mass-produced beef.

In response to growing public concern about the health effects of burgers and other fast-food fare, many restaurants began to offer healthier alternatives, such as turkey burgers, veggie burgers, and grilled chicken sandwiches. These menu options were marketed as lower in fat and calories than traditional burgers, appealing to health-conscious consumers looking for lighter, more nutritious meal options.

Despite these efforts to offer healthier alternatives, burgers continued to be associated with indulgence and excess, with their oversized portions, greasy toppings, and calorie-laden sides reinforcing their reputation as a guilty pleasure. With the rise of social media and food blogging in the 21st century, burgers became a popular subject of viral videos and Instagram-worthy photo shoots, with food enthusiasts seeking out the most outrageous and over-the-top burger creations to share with their followers.

In recent years, however, there has been a growing shift towards more mindful and balanced approaches to burger consumption, with consumers seeking out burgers made with high-quality, sustainably-sourced ingredients and served in moderation. Restaurants and food manufacturers have responded to this trend by offering healthier and more sustainable burger options, such as grass-fed beef, organic produce, and whole grain buns, appealing to consumers' desire for healthier and more environmentally-friendly choices.

Overall, perceptions of burger consumption have evolved significantly over time, reflecting changing attitudes towards diet, health, and food production. From their humble beginnings as a simple and affordable meal to their current status as a symbol of indulgence and excess, burgers have undergone a transformation in the public consciousness, shaped by cultural, social, and economic factors. While concerns about the health effects of burgers persist, there is also a growing recognition of their cultural significance and a renewed appreciation for burgers made with high-quality ingredients and served in moderation.

Nutritional Components of Burgers

Understanding the nutritional components of burgers is essential for making informed dietary choices and maintaining a balanced diet. While burgers are often associated with indulgence and excess, they can also be a source of important nutrients when prepared with high-quality ingredients and consumed in moderation. In this section, we'll explore the nutritional components of burgers, including their macronutrient content, micronutrient profile, and health implications.

Macronutrients are the three main components of food that provide energy: carbohydrates, proteins, and fats. Burgers typically contain all three macronutrients, although the proportions can vary depending on factors such as the type of meat used, the cooking method, and the choice of toppings and condiments.

Protein is a crucial macronutrient that plays a key role in building and repairing tissues, supporting immune function, and maintaining muscle mass. Burgers are an excellent source of protein, especially when made with lean cuts of meat such as chicken, turkey, or lean beef. Protein content can also be boosted by adding ingredients like beans, lentils, or tofu to the burger patty.

In addition to protein, burgers also provide carbohydrates, which are the body's primary source of energy. Carbohydrates are found in the bun and any added toppings such as lettuce, tomato, and onions. While burgers are not typically a significant source of carbohydrates, opting for whole grain buns or lettuce wraps can increase the fiber content and provide additional nutrients.

Fats are another important macronutrient found in burgers, primarily from the meat and any added cheese or condiments. While burgers can be high in saturated fats, which are associated with an increased risk of heart disease and other health problems, choosing lean cuts of meat and limiting added fats and oils can help to reduce the overall fat content of the burger.

Micronutrients are essential vitamins and minerals that are required in smaller amounts but play crucial roles in various physiological processes. While burgers are not typically a significant source of micronutrients, they can still contribute to overall nutrient intake, especially when prepared with nutrient-dense ingredients such as fresh vegetables and whole grain buns.

One of the primary micronutrients found in burgers is iron, which is important for oxygen transport, energy production, and immune function. Red meat, in particular, is a rich source of heme iron, which is more easily absorbed by the body than non-heme iron found in plant-based foods. However, excessive consumption of red meat has been linked to an increased risk of certain health problems, including heart disease and cancer, so it's important to enjoy burgers in moderation and opt for lean cuts of meat whenever possible.

Another important micronutrient found in burgers is zinc, which plays a key role in immune function, wound healing, and DNA synthesis. Beef is a particularly good source of zinc, although it can also be found in smaller amounts in other types of meat and plant-based proteins. Including a variety of protein sources in the diet can help to ensure an adequate intake of zinc and other essential nutrients.

Burgers can also provide a range of vitamins and minerals, depending on the ingredients used. For example, adding lettuce, tomato, and onions to a burger can increase its vitamin and mineral content, providing important nutrients such as vitamin C, vitamin K, and potassium. However, it's important to be mindful of added toppings and condiments that may be high in sodium, sugar, or unhealthy fats, as these can detract from the nutritional value of the burger.

While burgers can be a convenient and satisfying meal option, they can also be high in calories, saturated fats, and sodium, especially when prepared with processed meats and loaded with cheese, bacon, and other indulgent toppings. Consuming burgers in moderation and choosing healthier preparation methods, such as grilling or broiling instead of frying, can help to reduce their calorie and fat content while still enjoying their delicious flavor.

In conclusion, burgers can be a source of important nutrients when prepared with high-quality ingredients and consumed in moderation. Understanding the nutritional components of burgers, including their macronutrient content, micronutrient profile, and health implications, is essential for making informed dietary choices and maintaining a balanced diet. By choosing lean cuts of meat, opting for whole grain buns and plenty of fresh vegetables, and limiting added fats and condiments, burgers can be a delicious and nutritious addition to a healthy diet.

Health Concerns and Debates

Health concerns and debates surrounding burger consumption have become increasingly prominent in recent years, reflecting growing awareness of the potential health risks associated with diets high in saturated fats, sodium, and processed meats. While burgers are often enjoyed as a delicious and satisfying meal, they have also been the subject of controversy and debate among health experts, policymakers, and the general public. In this section, we'll explore some of the key health concerns and debates surrounding burger consumption, including their impact on heart health, obesity, and cancer risk, as well as the role of dietary guidelines and public health initiatives in promoting healthier eating habits.

One of the primary health concerns associated with burger consumption is their high content of saturated fats, which are known to raise levels of LDL cholesterol, or "bad" cholesterol, in the blood. Diets high in saturated fats have been linked to an increased risk of heart disease, stroke, and other cardiovascular problems, making them a major public health concern. Burgers made with fatty cuts of meat, processed meats such as bacon and sausage, and topped with cheese and other high-fat condiments can be particularly high in saturated fats, contributing to their negative impact on heart health.

In addition to their high saturated fat content, burgers can also be high in sodium, especially when prepared with processed meats and salty condiments such as pickles, ketchup, and mustard. Diets high in sodium have been linked to an increased risk of high blood pressure, heart disease, and stroke, making it important to monitor sodium intake and choose lower-sodium options whenever possible. Consuming burgers in moderation and opting for healthier preparation methods, such as grilling or broiling instead of frying, can help to reduce their sodium content and minimize their negative impact on cardiovascular health.

Another concern surrounding burger consumption is their potential role in promoting obesity and weight gain, particularly when consumed in excess or as part of a diet high in calories and unhealthy fats. Burgers are often served in oversized portions and accompanied by calorie-laden sides such as fries and soda, contributing to their high calorie content and potential for promoting weight gain. In addition, burgers are often marketed as indulgent and satisfying comfort foods, making them a popular choice for consumers looking for a quick and convenient meal option.

While burgers themselves are not inherently unhealthy, it's important to consider the context in which they are consumed and their overall contribution to the diet. Consuming burgers as an occasional treat or as part of a balanced diet that includes plenty of fruits, vegetables, whole grains, and lean proteins can help to minimize their negative impact on health and promote overall well-being. However, when consumed in excess or as part of a diet high in processed foods, burgers can contribute to weight gain, obesity, and other health problems.

One of the most contentious debates surrounding burger consumption is their potential role in increasing the risk of cancer, particularly colorectal cancer. Processed meats such as bacon, sausage, and hot dogs have been classified as Group 1 carcinogens by the International Agency for Research on Cancer (IARC), meaning that there is sufficient evidence to suggest that they can cause cancer in humans. Red meats such as beef, pork, and lamb have been classified as Group 2A carcinogens, meaning that they are probably carcinogenic to humans.

While the link between burger consumption and cancer risk is still the subject of ongoing research and debate, many health experts recommend limiting consumption of processed meats and red meats as part of a healthy diet to reduce the risk of cancer and other chronic diseases. This includes choosing lean cuts of meat, opting for plant-based proteins such as beans, lentils, and tofu, and incorporating plenty of fruits, vegetables, and whole grains into the diet.

Despite the health concerns and debates surrounding burger consumption, there is still room for burgers to be enjoyed as part of a healthy and balanced diet. By making informed choices about the types of meat and toppings used, opting for whole grain buns and plenty of fresh vegetables, and enjoying burgers in moderation, consumers can continue to enjoy this beloved comfort food while minimizing its negative impact on health.

In conclusion, burgers are a popular and iconic food choice enjoyed by millions of people around the world. However, they are also the subject of significant health concerns and debates, particularly regarding their impact on heart health, obesity, and cancer risk. While burgers can be enjoyed as part of a healthy and balanced diet, it's important to consider their overall contribution to the diet and to make informed choices about preparation methods and ingredients to minimize their negative impact on health. By choosing lean cuts of meat, opting for lower-sodium condiments, and enjoying burgers in moderation, consumers can continue to enjoy this beloved comfort food while promoting their overall well-being and longevity.

Rise of Plant-Based Alternatives

The rise of plant-based alternatives in the burger industry represents a significant shift in consumer preferences and dietary trends. As concerns about health, environmental sustainability, and animal welfare continue to grow, many consumers are seeking out plant-based alternatives to traditional meat burgers as a healthier, more sustainable, and ethically conscious option. In this section, we'll explore the factors driving the rise of plant-based alternatives, the nutritional benefits of plant-based burgers, and the impact of these alternatives on the burger industry and beyond.

One of the primary drivers behind the rise of plant-based alternatives is growing awareness of the health risks associated with excessive meat consumption. Research has linked high intake of red and processed meats to an increased risk of heart disease, cancer, and other chronic health conditions. As a result, many consumers are looking for healthier alternatives to traditional meat burgers that offer similar taste and texture without the negative health effects.

Plant-based burgers offer a solution to these health concerns by providing a cholesterol-free, lower-fat alternative to traditional meat burgers. Made from a combination of plant-based ingredients such as peas, beans, soy, and mushrooms, these burgers are rich in fiber, vitamins, minerals, and phytonutrients, making them a nutritious option for those looking to reduce their meat intake and improve their overall health.

In addition to their health benefits, plant-based burgers are also more environmentally sustainable than traditional meat burgers. The meat industry is a major contributor to greenhouse gas emissions, deforestation, water pollution, and other environmental problems. By choosing plant-based alternatives, consumers can reduce their environmental footprint and help to mitigate the negative impacts of industrial animal agriculture on the planet.

Another factor driving the rise of plant-based alternatives is concern for animal welfare. The meat industry is often criticized for its treatment of animals, including confinement in crowded and unsanitary conditions, use of hormones and antibiotics, and inhumane slaughter practices. Plant-based burgers offer a cruelty-free alternative to traditional meat burgers, allowing consumers to enjoy the taste and texture of burgers without the ethical concerns associated with animal agriculture.

The popularity of plant-based burgers has been further fueled by advances in food technology and innovation. Companies like Beyond Meat and Impossible Foods have developed plant-based burgers that closely mimic the taste, texture, and appearance of traditional meat burgers, making them appealing to both vegetarians and meat-eaters alike. These companies use techniques such as extrusion, fermentation, and flavoring to create burgers that sizzle, bleed, and taste like real meat, without the environmental and ethical drawbacks.

Plant-based burgers have also gained traction in the restaurant industry, with many fast-food chains and casual dining establishments adding them to their menus to meet growing consumer demand. Burger King, for example, introduced the Impossible Whopper, made with an Impossible Burger patty, to its menu in 2019, sparking widespread interest and media attention. Other chains, such as Carl's Jr., White Castle, and Dunkin', have also added plant-based burgers to their menus in response to consumer demand.

The rise of plant-based alternatives has not been without controversy, however, with some critics raising concerns about the healthfulness and nutritional adequacy of these products. While plant-based burgers are generally lower in saturated fat and cholesterol than traditional meat burgers, they can also be high in sodium, processed ingredients, and additives, which may detract from their nutritional value. Additionally, some plant-based burgers may be heavily processed and contain ingredients like soy protein isolate, pea protein concentrate, and methylcellulose, which may not be as wholesome or nutritious as whole plant foods.

There is also debate about the environmental sustainability of plant-based burgers, with some critics arguing that the production of plant-based ingredients like soy and peas can still have negative environmental impacts, including deforestation, habitat destruction, and pesticide use. Additionally, the processing and transportation of plant-based ingredients can also contribute to greenhouse gas emissions and other environmental problems, albeit to a lesser extent than industrial animal agriculture.

Despite these concerns, many experts agree that plant-based burgers can play a role in promoting a more sustainable and healthful diet, especially when consumed as part of a balanced and varied diet that includes plenty of fruits, vegetables, whole grains, and legumes. By choosing plant-based alternatives to traditional meat burgers, consumers can reduce their intake of saturated fat and cholesterol, increase their consumption of fiber and plant-based nutrients, and help to mitigate the environmental and ethical impacts of industrial animal agriculture.

In conclusion, the rise of plant-based alternatives in the burger industry represents a significant shift in consumer preferences and dietary trends, driven by concerns about health, environmental sustainability, and animal welfare. Plant-based burgers offer a cholesterol-free, lower-fat, and more environmentally sustainable alternative to traditional meat burgers, appealing to consumers looking for healthier, more ethical, and more sustainable options. While there are still debates and controversies surrounding the healthfulness, nutritional adequacy, and environmental sustainability of plant-based burgers, many experts agree that they can play a role in promoting a more sustainable and healthful diet when consumed as part of a balanced and varied plant-based diet.

Chapter 6: Social and Economic Impact
Urban Development and Burger Culture

Urban development and burger culture share a complex and intertwined relationship, with the evolution of cities often shaping the growth and proliferation of burger establishments, and in turn, burger culture influencing urban landscapes and social dynamics. From the emergence of the first diners in bustling metropolises to the rise of trendy burger joints in gentrifying neighborhoods, the urban environment has played a central role in shaping the way people experience and interact with burgers. In this section, we'll explore the multifaceted relationship between urban development and burger culture, examining how factors such as demographics, economics, and social trends have influenced the urban burger landscape.

The evolution of burger culture in urban environments can be traced back to the early 20th century, when diners and drive-ins began to proliferate in bustling cities across the United States. These establishments served as affordable and accessible dining options for urban workers and residents, offering a taste of comfort and nostalgia in the midst of the fast-paced urban landscape. As cities grew and expanded, so too did the demand for convenient and affordable dining options, leading to the proliferation of burger joints in urban neighborhoods.

One of the key drivers of urban development and burger culture is demographic change, with shifts in population density, income levels, and cultural diversity shaping the demand for burgers and influencing the types of establishments that thrive in urban environments. In cities with diverse populations, burger joints often cater to a wide range of tastes and preferences, offering everything from classic diner-style burgers to gourmet creations inspired by global cuisines. This diversity of options reflects the rich tapestry of urban life and the vibrant culinary landscape of cities around the world.

Economic factors also play a significant role in shaping the urban burger landscape, with factors such as real estate prices, labor costs, and consumer spending habits influencing the types of burger establishments that can thrive in urban environments. In cities where rents are high and competition is fierce, burger joints often need to differentiate themselves by offering unique menu items, innovative dining experiences, or exceptional service in order to attract and retain customers. This competitive environment can lead to the emergence of trendy burger joints that cater to urban foodies and culinary enthusiasts, as well as established diners and drive-ins that have stood the test of time.

Social trends and cultural movements also influence the urban burger landscape, with factors such as health consciousness, environmental awareness, and ethical concerns shaping consumer preferences and driving demand for alternative burger options. In recent years, there has been a growing interest in plant-based and vegan burgers, driven by concerns about animal welfare, environmental sustainability, and personal health. As a result, many urban burger joints have begun to offer plant-based burger options made from ingredients such as tofu, seitan, and legumes, appealing to a new generation of health-conscious and environmentally-conscious consumers.

The rise of food delivery services and online ordering platforms has also had a significant impact on the urban burger landscape, with many burger joints adapting to meet the demands of a digital-savvy customer base. In cities where delivery is popular and dining out is less common, burger joints often invest in technology and infrastructure to streamline the ordering and delivery process, ensuring that customers can enjoy their favorite burgers wherever they are. This shift towards convenience and accessibility reflects the changing lifestyles and preferences of urban residents, who increasingly value convenience and flexibility in their dining experiences.

Gentrification and urban renewal projects can also influence the urban burger landscape, with new developments and revitalized neighborhoods often attracting trendy restaurants and upscale burger joints catering to affluent residents and visitors. While gentrification can bring economic opportunities and cultural vibrancy to urban areas, it can also lead to displacement and social tensions, with long-time residents feeling marginalized or excluded from the benefits of development. As a result, the relationship between gentrification and burger culture is complex and multifaceted, with both positive and negative implications for urban communities.

In conclusion, the relationship between urban development and burger culture is complex and multifaceted, with factors such as demographics, economics, social trends, and cultural movements shaping the urban burger landscape in dynamic ways. From the emergence of diners and drive-ins in bustling metropolises to the rise of trendy burger joints in gentrifying neighborhoods, burgers have become an integral part of urban life, reflecting the diversity, vibrancy, and complexity of the urban environment. As cities continue to evolve and change, so too will the urban burger landscape, with new trends, innovations, and cultural influences shaping the way people experience and interact with burgers in the cities of tomorrow.

Job Creation and Economic Influence

Job creation and economic influence are significant aspects of the social and economic impact of the burger industry. Burgers have not only become a staple of the American diet but also a significant driver of economic activity, providing employment opportunities and contributing to local economies through restaurant sales, supply chain activities, and related industries. In this section, we'll explore the role of burger joints in job creation and economic influence, examining how they contribute to employment growth, stimulate consumer spending, and support broader economic development efforts.

One of the primary ways in which burger joints contribute to the economy is through job creation. The burger industry is a major employer, providing jobs for millions of workers across the country in various roles such as chefs, cooks, servers, cashiers, managers, and support staff. From fast-food chains to upscale burger joints, burger establishments offer a diverse range of employment opportunities that cater to individuals with varying skill levels, education levels, and experience.

The burger industry is known for its relatively low barriers to entry, making it accessible to individuals from diverse backgrounds and demographics. Many burger joints offer entry-level positions that require minimal training or experience, making them attractive options for young people, students, and individuals entering the workforce for the first time. These jobs provide valuable opportunities for skill development, career advancement, and financial stability, serving as a stepping stone to higher-paying and more rewarding positions in the restaurant industry and beyond.

In addition to providing entry-level employment opportunities, burger joints also offer opportunities for career advancement and professional growth. Many burger chains and independent restaurants offer training programs, apprenticeships, and mentorship opportunities to help employees develop valuable skills, gain industry certifications, and advance their careers within the company. For example, employees may start as line cooks or cashiers and work their way up to management positions or even franchise ownership, demonstrating the potential for upward mobility and success within the burger industry.

The economic influence of burger joints extends beyond job creation to include a wide range of economic activities that support local economies and stimulate growth. Burger joints contribute to economic development by generating sales revenue, paying taxes, and supporting local suppliers, vendors, and service providers. For example, burger joints purchase ingredients, equipment, and supplies from local farmers, ranchers, and food distributors, supporting agricultural production and distribution networks in the communities where they operate.

Furthermore, burger joints stimulate consumer spending and drive foot traffic to commercial districts, shopping centers, and entertainment venues, contributing to the vibrancy and vitality of local economies. Whether it's grabbing a quick burger on a lunch break, meeting friends for dinner at a neighborhood burger joint, or enjoying a meal with family at a favorite burger restaurant, burgers are a popular dining option that attracts customers of all ages and backgrounds, driving demand for goods and services in the surrounding area.

The economic impact of burger joints is especially pronounced in urban areas, where the density of restaurants and the concentration of consumers create a fertile ground for economic activity. In cities with vibrant dining scenes, burger joints play a central role in shaping the character and identity of neighborhoods, contributing to the cultural fabric and social dynamics of urban life. From trendy burger bars in gentrifying neighborhoods to classic diners in historic districts, burger joints are often anchors of community life, providing gathering spaces where people can come together to eat, socialize, and connect.

Moreover, burger joints are often important contributors to tourism and hospitality industries, attracting visitors from near and far who come to sample the local culinary scene and experience the unique flavors and traditions of different regions. Burger festivals, food tours, and culinary events draw crowds of food enthusiasts and travelers eager to taste the latest burger creations, driving revenue for local businesses and generating positive publicity for the destination.

In conclusion, burger joints play a significant role in job creation and economic influence, providing employment opportunities, stimulating consumer spending, and supporting broader economic development efforts. From fast-food chains to upscale burger bars, burger establishments contribute to local economies through restaurant sales, supply chain activities, and related industries. By creating jobs, generating revenue, and fostering economic growth, burger joints play a vital role in shaping the social and economic fabric of communities across the country.

Burger Tourism and Travel Destinations

Burger tourism and travel destinations have emerged as a popular trend in recent years, as food enthusiasts and travelers seek out iconic burger joints, gourmet burger bars, and unique burger creations in cities and towns around the world. From classic diners and drive-ins to celebrity chef-owned restaurants and innovative food trucks, burger establishments have become destinations in their own right, drawing visitors from near and far who come to sample the local burger culture and experience the unique flavors and traditions of different regions. In this section, we'll explore the phenomenon of burger tourism and travel destinations, examining how burger joints have become must-visit attractions for food lovers and tourists alike.

One of the key drivers of burger tourism is the rise of food tourism and culinary travel, with more people traveling specifically to experience the local food scene and sample regional specialties. Burgers, with their universal appeal and wide range of variations, have become a focal point of food tourism, attracting visitors who want to taste the best burgers a destination has to offer and explore the unique flavors and techniques that define burger culture in different regions.

Burger tourism is often driven by a desire to experience the authentic flavors and traditions of a destination, whether it's sampling regional specialties like the famous Juicy Lucy in Minneapolis, the legendary Jucy Lucy in Minneapolis, the iconic In-N-Out Burger in California, or the innovative ramen burger in New York City. Many burger enthusiasts are willing to travel long distances and wait in line for hours to taste these iconic creations and experience the atmosphere and ambiance of the establishments that serve them.

In addition to iconic burger joints, burger tourism also encompasses a wide range of culinary experiences, including burger festivals, food tours, and culinary events that celebrate the diverse and dynamic world of burgers. From the annual Burger Fest in Chicago to the World Burger Championship in Las Vegas, these events attract thousands of attendees who come to sample burgers from top chefs, food trucks, and restaurants, participate in cooking competitions, and celebrate their love of all things burger-related.

Burger tourism is also fueled by the rise of social media and food blogging, with influencers and bloggers sharing their burger adventures with followers around the world, inspiring others to seek out the best burgers in their own travels. Instagram-worthy burger creations, viral videos of over-the-top burger challenges, and mouthwatering burger photos posted on social media platforms like Instagram, Facebook, and TikTok have helped to elevate the status of burgers as a cultural phenomenon and fuel the desire to experience them firsthand.

One of the most iconic destinations for burger tourism is the United States, home to a rich and diverse burger culture that reflects the country's melting pot of culinary influences and traditions. From the classic diner-style burgers of the Midwest to the gourmet creations of coastal cities like Los Angeles and New York, the United States offers a wide range of burger experiences for travelers to explore and enjoy.

Cities like New York City, Los Angeles, Chicago, and Austin have become hotspots for burger tourism, with vibrant dining scenes and a wealth of burger joints catering to every taste and preference. From hole-in-the-wall burger dives to trendy burger bars and celebrity chef-owned restaurants, these cities offer a diverse range of burger experiences that showcase the creativity, innovation, and diversity of American burger culture.

In addition to the United States, burger tourism is also popular in other countries around the world, with destinations like Japan, Australia, and the United Kingdom attracting burger enthusiasts who want to experience the unique twists and variations of burgers in different cultures. Whether it's the Wagyu beef burgers of Japan, the kangaroo burgers of Australia, or the gourmet brioche burgers of the UK, each destination offers its own take on the beloved burger, providing travelers with a taste of the local culinary scene and a memorable dining experience.

Burger tourism not only provides opportunities for travelers to explore new flavors and culinary traditions but also contributes to local economies through tourism spending, restaurant sales, and related industries. Burger joints that attract tourists can benefit from increased visibility, foot traffic, and revenue, helping to support their growth and success in an increasingly competitive market.

In conclusion, burger tourism and travel destinations have become a popular trend in recent years, as food enthusiasts and travelers seek out iconic burger joints, gourmet burger bars, and unique burger creations in cities and towns around the world. Whether it's sampling regional specialties, attending burger festivals, or exploring the diverse and dynamic world of burgers, burger tourism offers travelers a unique opportunity to experience the local culinary scene and immerse themselves in the rich and vibrant world of burger culture.

Corporate Influence and Big Burger Brands

Corporate influence and big burger brands wield significant power and influence in the global food industry, shaping consumer preferences, driving market trends, and influencing the way burgers are produced, marketed, and consumed. From multinational fast-food chains to global food conglomerates, these corporate giants play a central role in shaping the social and economic landscape of the burger industry, impacting everything from food policy and public health to labor practices and environmental sustainability. In this section, we'll explore the corporate influence and big burger brands, examining how these industry players have transformed the burger industry and the broader implications for society, economy, and the environment.

One of the defining characteristics of the modern burger industry is the dominance of multinational fast-food chains, which have become synonymous with burgers and fast-food culture around the world. Companies like McDonald's, Burger King, and Wendy's have achieved global recognition and success, with thousands of restaurants operating in countries across every continent, serving millions of customers each day. These fast-food giants have revolutionized the way burgers are produced, marketed, and consumed, introducing innovations like the drive-thru, the Happy Meal, and the dollar menu that have reshaped the fast-food landscape and transformed the dining habits of consumers worldwide.

Fast-food chains are known for their standardized menu offerings, efficient production processes, and aggressive marketing strategies, which prioritize convenience, affordability, and consistency over quality and nutritional value. Burgers served at fast-food chains are often made with highly processed ingredients, artificial additives, and preservatives, which can contribute to health problems such as obesity, diabetes, and heart disease when consumed in excess. Despite these concerns, fast-food chains continue to attract customers with their low prices, convenient locations, and ubiquitous advertising campaigns, making them a dominant force in the global burger industry.

In addition to fast-food chains, big burger brands also include global food conglomerates that own and operate multiple restaurant chains and food brands, spanning a wide range of cuisines and dining concepts. Companies like Yum! Brands, Restaurant Brands International, and The Wendy's Company own and operate a portfolio of burger chains, fast-food franchises, and casual dining restaurants, leveraging their scale and resources to drive growth, expand market share, and increase profitability.

The rise of big burger brands has led to concerns about corporate consolidation and market concentration, with a small number of companies controlling a large share of the global burger market. This concentration of power can stifle competition, limit consumer choice, and reduce innovation, as smaller, independent burger joints struggle to compete with the marketing budgets, economies of scale, and brand recognition of big burger brands. Moreover, the dominance of big burger brands can have negative implications for food quality, public health, and environmental sustainability, as companies prioritize profits over the well-being of consumers, workers, and the planet.

One of the key challenges associated with corporate influence and big burger brands is the impact on public health and nutrition. Fast-food chains and big burger brands have been criticized for their role in promoting unhealthy eating habits, contributing to rising rates of obesity, diabetes, and other diet-related diseases. Burgers served at fast-food chains are often high in calories, saturated fat, and sodium, with little nutritional value beyond their energy content. While some chains have introduced healthier menu options in response to consumer demand and regulatory pressure, these efforts are often overshadowed by the continued popularity of classic burger offerings and indulgent menu items.

In addition to concerns about public health, corporate influence and big burger brands also raise questions about labor practices and worker rights. Fast-food workers are often paid low wages, receive minimal benefits, and face precarious working conditions, leading to high turnover rates, labor disputes, and protests for higher wages and better working conditions. Despite these challenges, fast-food chains continue to rely on a large and diverse workforce to operate their restaurants, with millions of employees working in roles ranging from front-line service to corporate management.

Another area of concern is the environmental impact of corporate influence and big burger brands, particularly in terms of resource consumption, waste generation, and greenhouse gas emissions. The production of beef, the primary ingredient in most burgers served at fast-food chains and big burger brands, is a major driver of deforestation, habitat destruction, and biodiversity loss, as forests are cleared to make way for pastureland and feed crops. Moreover, the intensive farming practices used to raise beef cattle, including feedlot operations, water usage, and methane emissions, contribute to climate change and environmental degradation, further exacerbating the ecological footprint of burgers.

Despite these challenges, some big burger brands have taken steps to address environmental concerns and promote sustainability in their operations. Initiatives such as sustainable sourcing, waste reduction, and energy efficiency are increasingly being adopted by fast-food chains and big burger brands in response to consumer demand, investor pressure, and regulatory requirements. For example, some companies have committed to sourcing beef from suppliers that adhere to strict environmental and animal welfare standards, investing in renewable energy and carbon offsets, and reducing packaging waste and single-use plastics in their restaurants.

In conclusion, corporate influence and big burger brands play a significant role in shaping the social, economic, and environmental dimensions of the burger industry, impacting everything from public health and nutrition to labor practices and environmental sustainability. While fast-food chains and big burger brands have revolutionized the way burgers are produced, marketed, and consumed, they also face criticism and scrutiny for their role in promoting unhealthy eating habits, exploiting workers, and contributing to environmental degradation. As consumers become more conscious of the social and environmental implications of their food choices, there is growing pressure on big burger brands to adopt more sustainable and responsible practices that prioritize the well-being of people, animals, and the planet.

Chapter 7: Culinary Techniques and Recipes
Choosing the Right Meat and Ingredients

Choosing the right meat and ingredients is crucial in creating the perfect burger, as they form the foundation of its flavor, texture, and overall quality. From selecting the type of meat to choosing the freshest produce and condiments, every ingredient plays a vital role in crafting a burger that is flavorful, juicy, and satisfying. In this section, we'll explore the importance of choosing the right meat and ingredients for burgers, examining different types of meats, cuts, and toppings, as well as tips and techniques for maximizing flavor and freshness.

At the heart of every burger is the meat, and choosing the right type and quality of meat is essential for creating a delicious and satisfying burger. While beef is the most traditional and popular choice for burgers, other meats such as chicken, turkey, pork, and even plant-based alternatives are also used to create a wide range of burger variations to suit different tastes and dietary preferences.

When it comes to beef, the choice of meat can greatly impact the flavor, juiciness, and texture of the burger. Ground beef is the most common choice for burgers, with varying levels of fat content ranging from lean (such as 90/10 or 85/15) to medium (such as 80/20) to fatty (such as 70/30). The fat content of the meat affects the juiciness and tenderness of the burger, with higher fat content resulting in a juicier and more flavorful burger, while leaner cuts may be drier and less tender.

In addition to fat content, the type of beef used can also influence the flavor and quality of the burger. Different cuts of beef, such as chuck, sirloin, brisket, and short rib, offer unique flavors and textures that can be combined to create a custom blend that suits your preferences. Many burger aficionados prefer a blend of multiple cuts, as this allows for a balance of flavor, juiciness, and tenderness that is not achievable with a single cut alone.

When selecting beef for burgers, it's important to choose high-quality, freshly ground meat from a reputable butcher or grocery store. Look for meat that is bright red in color, with marbling throughout the meat for added flavor and juiciness. Avoid meat that appears gray or brown in color or has a strong odor, as this may indicate spoilage or improper handling.

In addition to beef, other meats such as chicken, turkey, pork, and even seafood can be used to create delicious and unique burgers. Chicken and turkey burgers offer a leaner alternative to beef, with a lighter flavor and texture that pairs well with a variety of toppings and seasonings. Pork burgers, often made from ground pork shoulder or loin, are rich and flavorful, with a slightly sweet and savory taste that pairs well with bold flavors like barbecue sauce and spicy condiments.

For those looking for a plant-based alternative, there are now a variety of plant-based burger patties available on the market made from ingredients such as soy, pea protein, mushrooms, and beets. These plant-based burgers offer a meat-like texture and flavor that closely resembles traditional beef burgers, making them a popular choice for vegetarians, vegans, and flexitarians looking to reduce their meat consumption without sacrificing taste or texture.

In addition to choosing the right type and quality of meat, selecting fresh and flavorful ingredients is essential for creating a delicious and satisfying burger. From the bun to the toppings, every ingredient should be carefully chosen to complement the flavors and textures of the meat and enhance the overall eating experience.

The bun is an often overlooked but essential component of the burger, providing a sturdy base for holding the meat and toppings while adding flavor and texture to each bite. While traditional hamburger buns are made from white flour, there are now a variety of bun options available, including whole wheat, brioche, pretzel, and gluten-free options, each offering its own unique flavor and texture profile. When choosing a bun, look for one that is soft and fresh, with a slightly sweet and buttery flavor that complements the savory taste of the burger.

When it comes to toppings, the possibilities are endless, with a wide range of options to suit every taste and preference. Classic burger toppings such as lettuce, tomato, onion, and pickles add freshness and crunch to each bite, while more adventurous toppings like avocado, bacon, fried eggs, and caramelized onions can elevate the flavor and texture of the burger to new heights. Experiment with different combinations of toppings to find your perfect burger recipe, and don't be afraid to get creative with flavors and textures.

Condiments are another important element of the burger experience, adding moisture, flavor, and tanginess to each bite. Classic condiments such as ketchup, mustard, and mayonnaise are popular choices for burgers, while specialty sauces like barbecue sauce, aioli, and hot sauce can add a unique twist to the flavor profile. Experiment with different combinations of condiments to find your perfect burger sauce, and don't be afraid to try new flavors and ingredients to customize your burger to your taste.

In addition to traditional toppings and condiments, there are also a variety of specialty ingredients that can be used to add flavor and texture to burgers. Cheese is a classic burger topping that adds richness and creaminess to each bite, with popular options including cheddar, American, Swiss, and blue cheese. Other specialty ingredients such as caramelized onions, sautéed mushrooms, avocado, and bacon can add depth and complexity to the flavor profile of the burger, creating a truly unforgettable dining experience.

In conclusion, choosing the right meat and ingredients is essential for creating a delicious and satisfying burger. From selecting the type and quality of meat to choosing fresh and flavorful toppings and condiments, every ingredient plays a vital role in crafting the perfect burger. Experiment with different combinations of meats, cuts, and toppings to find your perfect burger recipe, and don't be afraid to get creative with flavors and textures. Whether you prefer a classic cheeseburger with lettuce, tomato, and onion or a gourmet creation with avocado, bacon, and blue cheese, the key to a great burger is choosing the right meat and ingredients to suit your taste and preferences.

Cooking Methods and Grilling Techniques

Cooking methods and grilling techniques are essential aspects of creating the perfect burger, as they influence the flavor, texture, and juiciness of the meat while imparting delicious charred notes and smoky aromas. From traditional grilling methods to alternative cooking techniques, mastering the art of burger cooking requires an understanding of the principles of heat transfer, timing, and temperature control. In this section, we'll explore various cooking methods and grilling techniques for burgers, including tips and tricks for achieving perfectly cooked burgers every time.

Grilling is perhaps the most popular and iconic method of cooking burgers, as it allows for direct exposure to high heat, resulting in delicious charred crusts and juicy interiors. Whether using a gas grill, charcoal grill, or electric grill, the key to successful grilling is proper temperature control and timing. Preheat the grill to medium-high heat (around 375-400°F) for optimal grilling conditions, and make sure the grates are clean and well-oiled to prevent sticking.

When grilling burgers, it's important to start with high-quality meat and properly shaped patties that are uniform in size and thickness. This ensures even cooking and prevents unevenly cooked burgers. Season the patties generously with salt and pepper just before placing them on the grill to maximize flavor, and avoid overhandling the meat to prevent it from becoming tough and dry.

Once the grill is hot and the patties are seasoned, place them directly over the heat source and cook for approximately

4-5 minutes per side for medium-rare burgers, or longer if desired. Avoid pressing down on the patties with a spatula, as this can release juices and result in dry burgers. Instead, flip the patties once halfway through cooking to ensure even browning and caramelization on both sides.

For those who prefer a smokier flavor, adding wood chips or chunks to the grill can impart delicious smoky aromas to the burgers. Simply soak the wood chips in water for 30 minutes before placing them in a smoker box or aluminum foil packet on the grill. The wood chips will slowly smolder and release smoke, infusing the burgers with rich, complex flavors that complement the charred crust and juicy interior.

Another popular grilling technique for burgers is the "reverse sear" method, which involves cooking the burgers at a low temperature before finishing them over high heat to sear the exterior. This method helps to ensure even cooking and optimal juiciness, as the low heat gently cooks the burgers to the desired doneness without overcooking the exterior.

To use the reverse sear method, preheat the grill to low heat (around 225-250°F) and place the seasoned patties on the indirect heat side of the grill. Close the lid and cook the burgers for approximately 20-30 minutes, or until they reach an internal temperature of 120-125°F for medium-rare. Once the burgers are cooked to the desired doneness, transfer them to the direct heat side of the grill and sear them for 1-2 minutes per side, or until they develop a golden-brown crust.

In addition to traditional grilling methods, there are also alternative cooking techniques for burgers that can yield delicious results. One such method is pan-searing, which involves cooking the burgers in a hot skillet or frying pan on the stovetop. Pan-searing allows for even browning and caramelization, resulting in burgers that are crispy on the outside and juicy on the inside.

To pan-sear burgers, heat a skillet or frying pan over medium-high heat and add a small amount of oil or butter to prevent sticking. Once the pan is hot, add the seasoned patties and cook for approximately 3-4 minutes per side, or until they develop a golden-brown crust and reach the desired level of doneness. For added flavor, you can deglaze the pan with a splash of wine, broth, or beer and use the drippings to make a delicious pan sauce to serve with the burgers.

Another alternative cooking technique for burgers is baking, which involves cooking the patties in the oven instead of on the grill or stovetop. Baking is a convenient option for those who don't have access to a grill or prefer a hands-off approach to cooking. To bake burgers, preheat the oven to 400°F and place the seasoned patties on a baking sheet lined with parchment paper or aluminum foil. Bake for approximately 15-20 minutes, or until the burgers reach an internal temperature of 160°F for medium doneness.

In conclusion, mastering the art of burger cooking requires an understanding of various cooking methods and grilling techniques, each of which offers unique advantages and flavors. Whether grilling over an open flame, pan-searing on the stovetop, or baking in the oven, the key to delicious burgers lies in proper temperature control, timing, and seasoning.

Experiment with different cooking methods and techniques to find your perfect burger recipe, and don't be afraid to get creative with flavors and toppings to suit your taste and preferences.

Secret Sauce Recipes and Burger Hacks

Secret sauce recipes and burger hacks are essential components of creating memorable and irresistible burgers that stand out from the crowd. These special sauces and innovative techniques elevate the flavor profile of burgers, adding layers of complexity, richness, and tanginess that tantalize the taste buds and leave a lasting impression on diners. In this section, we'll explore some secret sauce recipes and burger hacks that will take your burger game to the next level, providing tips and tricks for creating mouthwatering burgers that are sure to impress.

One of the most iconic and beloved secret sauce recipes in the world of burgers is the classic "special sauce," made famous by fast-food chains like McDonald's and Big Mac. This tangy and creamy sauce is the perfect accompaniment to burgers, adding a burst of flavor and richness that enhances the overall eating experience. While the exact recipe for special sauce is closely guarded by these fast-food giants, there are many homemade versions that replicate the taste and texture of the original.

To make your own special sauce at home, start with a base of mayonnaise and add ketchup, mustard, sweet pickle relish, and vinegar to taste. You can also add additional ingredients such as finely minced onion, garlic powder, paprika, and Worcestershire sauce for extra flavor and depth. Mix the ingredients together in a bowl until well combined, then refrigerate the sauce for at least an hour to allow the flavors to meld together. Serve the special sauce alongside burgers as a dipping sauce or spread it directly on the buns for a deliciously decadent treat.

In addition to special sauce, there are many other secret sauce recipes that can take your burgers to the next level. From tangy barbecue sauce to zesty aioli to spicy chipotle mayo, the possibilities are endless when it comes to creating custom sauces for burgers. Experiment with different flavor combinations and ingredients to find your perfect sauce recipe, and don't be afraid to get creative with bold flavors and unexpected pairings.

Another secret sauce that adds a unique twist to burgers is the Japanese-inspired "teriyaki mayo," made with a blend of soy sauce, mirin, sake, and mayonnaise. This savory and slightly sweet sauce pairs beautifully with grilled burgers, adding a delicious umami flavor and a hint of sweetness that complements the charred crust and juicy interior of the meat. To make teriyaki mayo, simply whisk together equal parts soy sauce, mirin, and sake in a small saucepan and bring to a simmer over medium heat. Cook until the mixture has reduced by half, then let it cool completely before stirring in mayonnaise until smooth and creamy. Drizzle the teriyaki mayo over burgers or use it as a dipping sauce for an extra burst of flavor.

In addition to secret sauce recipes, there are also many burger hacks and tips that can help you create perfect burgers every time. One popular burger hack is the "smash burger" technique, which involves pressing the burger patties flat against the cooking surface to create a thin and crispy crust while retaining juiciness and flavor. To make smash burgers, form the ground beef into small balls and place them on a hot griddle or skillet. Use a sturdy spatula to press down firmly on each patty, flattening them into thin discs. Cook the patties for 2-3 minutes on each side, or until they develop a golden-brown crust and are cooked to the desired level of doneness. Serve the smash burgers on toasted buns with your favorite toppings and condiments for a deliciously indulgent treat.

Another burger hack that can take your burgers to the next level is the "stuffed burger" technique, which involves adding flavorful fillings and toppings inside the burger patty for an extra burst of flavor and texture. To make stuffed burgers, divide the ground beef into equal portions and form them into thin patties. Place your desired fillings, such as cheese, bacon, caramelized onions, or mushrooms, in the center of half of the patties, then place the remaining patties on top and seal the edges to encase the fillings. Cook the stuffed burgers on the grill or stovetop until they are cooked through and the fillings are melted and gooey. Serve the stuffed burgers on toasted buns with additional toppings and condiments for a deliciously indulgent meal that is sure to impress.

In addition to secret sauce recipes and burger hacks, there are also many tips and tricks for maximizing flavor and juiciness when cooking burgers. One important tip is to avoid overhandling the meat, as this can compact the patties and result in tough, dry burgers. Instead, gently shape the ground beef into patties and make a slight indentation in the center of each patty with your thumb to prevent it from puffing up during cooking. This will ensure that the burgers cook evenly and retain their juiciness and tenderness.

Another tip for creating perfect burgers is to cook them to the desired level of doneness using a meat thermometer to ensure accuracy. For medium-rare burgers, cook the patties until they reach an internal temperature of 130-135°F, while for medium burgers, cook them until they reach 140-145°F. Remember that the burgers will continue to cook slightly after they are removed from the heat, so it's important to take them off the grill or stovetop slightly before they reach the desired temperature.

In conclusion, secret sauce recipes and burger hacks are essential components of creating delicious and memorable burgers that stand out from the crowd. Whether you're making homemade special sauce, experimenting with unique flavor combinations, or trying out innovative cooking techniques, there are endless opportunities to elevate the flavor and quality of your burgers. With a little creativity and experimentation, you can create mouthwatering burgers that are sure to impress friends and family alike.

Signature Burgers from Around the World

Signature burgers from around the world offer a tantalizing glimpse into the diverse and flavorful culinary traditions of different cultures and regions. From classic American cheeseburgers to exotic creations inspired by global cuisines, these burgers showcase the creativity and innovation of chefs and home cooks alike. In this section, we'll take a culinary journey around the world to explore some of the most iconic and mouthwatering signature burgers from various countries and cultures.

1. The Juicy Lucy - United States: Originating from Minneapolis, Minnesota, the Juicy Lucy is a legendary burger known for its oozing center of melted cheese. This iconic creation features two beef patties sandwiched together with a generous amount of cheese stuffed inside, creating a molten core of gooey goodness when bitten into. The Juicy Lucy is typically served on a soft bun with classic toppings like lettuce, tomato, and onion, but the real star of the show is the molten cheese filling that bursts with every bite.

2. The Ramen Burger - Japan: A fusion of East and West, the Ramen Burger is a quirky and inventive creation that has taken the culinary world by storm. This Japanese-inspired burger features a beef patty sandwiched between two crispy ramen noodle "buns," which are made by molding cooked ramen noodles into bun shapes and then frying them until golden and crispy. The result is a unique combination of textures and flavors, with the savory umami of the beef patty complemented by the crunchy texture of the ramen noodles.

3. The Bánh Mì Burger - Vietnam: Inspired by the traditional Vietnamese sandwich of the same name, the Bánh Mì Burger combines the bold flavors of Vietnamese cuisine with the classic elements of a burger. This fusion creation features a juicy beef patty topped with pickled vegetables, fresh cilantro, spicy jalapenos, and tangy mayonnaise, all served on a toasted bánh mì bun. The combination of sweet, savory, spicy, and tangy flavors makes this burger a deliciously unique culinary experience.

4. The Kangaroo Burger - Australia: A true taste of the Outback, the Kangaroo Burger is a quintessentially Australian creation that showcases the country's unique culinary heritage. Made from lean kangaroo meat, which is low in fat and high in protein, this burger offers a healthy and sustainable alternative to traditional beef burgers. The kangaroo meat is typically seasoned with native Australian spices and grilled to perfection, then served on a toasted bun with classic toppings like lettuce, tomato, and onion.

5. The Kofta Burger - Middle East: A staple of Middle Eastern cuisine, the Kofta Burger is a flavorful and aromatic burger that is packed with spices and herbs. The burger patty is made from seasoned ground lamb or beef, mixed with onions, garlic, parsley, and a blend of Middle Eastern spices such as cumin, coriander, and cinnamon. The patties are then grilled or pan-seared until golden and juicy, and served on a warm pita bread with creamy tahini sauce, fresh cucumber, and tomato slices.

6. The Galbi Burger - South Korea: Combining the flavors of traditional Korean barbecue with the convenience of a burger, the Galbi Burger is a mouthwatering fusion creation that has gained popularity both in South Korea and around the world. This burger features a beef patty marinated in a sweet and savory sauce made from soy sauce, sugar, garlic, and sesame oil, then grilled to perfection and served on a toasted bun with crisp lettuce, pickled radishes, and spicy gochujang sauce.

7. The Jucy Lucy - United States: Originating from Minneapolis, Minnesota, the Jucy Lucy is a legendary burger known for its oozing center of melted cheese. This iconic creation features two beef patties sandwiched together with a generous amount of cheese stuffed inside, creating a molten core of gooey goodness when bitten into. The Jucy Lucy is typically served on a soft bun with classic toppings like lettuce, tomato, and onion, but the real star of the show is the molten cheese filling that bursts with every bite.

8. The Ramen Burger - Japan: A fusion of East and West, the Ramen Burger is a quirky and inventive creation that has taken the culinary world by storm. This Japanese-inspired burger features a beef patty sandwiched between two crispy ramen noodle "buns," which are made by molding cooked ramen noodles into bun shapes and then frying them until golden and crispy. The result is a unique combination of textures and flavors, with the savory umami of the beef patty complemented by the crunchy texture of the ramen noodles.

9. The Bánh Mì Burger - Vietnam: Inspired by the traditional Vietnamese sandwich of the same name, the Bánh Mì Burger combines the bold flavors of Vietnamese cuisine with the classic elements of a burger. This fusion creation features a juicy beef patty topped with pickled vegetables, fresh cilantro, spicy jalapenos, and tangy mayonnaise, all served on a toasted bánh mì bun. The combination of sweet, savory, spicy, and tangy flavors makes this burger a deliciously unique culinary experience.

10. The Kangaroo Burger - Australia: A true taste of the Outback, the Kangaroo Burger is a quintessentially Australian creation that showcases the country's unique culinary heritage. Made from lean kangaroo meat, which is low in fat and high in protein, this burger offers a healthy and sustainable alternative to traditional beef burgers. The kangaroo meat is typically seasoned with native Australian spices and grilled to perfection, then served on a toasted bun with classic toppings like lettuce, tomato, and onion.

11. The Kofta Burger - Middle East: A staple of Middle Eastern cuisine, the Kofta Burger is a flavorful and aromatic burger that is packed with spices and herbs. The burger patty is made from seasoned ground lamb or beef, mixed with onions, garlic, parsley, and a blend of Middle Eastern spices such as cumin, coriander, and cinnamon. The patties are then grilled or pan-seared until golden and juicy, and served on a warm pita bread with creamy tahini sauce, fresh cucumber, and tomato slices.

12. The Galbi Burger - South Korea: Combining the flavors of traditional Korean barbecue with the convenience of a burger, the Galbi Burger is a mouthwatering fusion creation that has gained popularity both in South Korea and around the world. This burger features a beef patty marinated in a sweet and savory sauce made from soy sauce, sugar, garlic, and sesame oil, then grilled to perfection and served on a toasted bun with crisp lettuce, pickled radishes, and spicy gochujang sauce.

In conclusion, signature burgers from around the world offer a delicious and diverse culinary experience that reflects the unique flavors and ingredients of different cultures and regions. From classic American cheeseburgers to exotic creations inspired by global cuisines, these burgers showcase the creativity and innovation of chefs and home cooks alike, providing a tantalizing glimpse into the rich tapestry of the world's culinary heritage.

Chapter 8: Pop Culture References
Burger in Film and Television

Burgers have left an indelible mark on popular culture, and their presence in film and television is a testament to their iconic status in society. From heartwarming scenes set in classic diners to fast-food feuds and larger-than-life burger challenges, burgers have played a variety of roles in shaping memorable moments on the big and small screens. In this section, we'll explore the rich and diverse portrayal of burgers in film and television, examining their significance as both a prop and a symbol in storytelling.

Burgers as a Symbol of American Culture: In many films and television shows, burgers serve as a symbol of American culture, representing concepts such as comfort, nostalgia, and the pursuit of the American dream. Classic diner scenes featuring characters enjoying burgers and milkshakes evoke a sense of nostalgia for a bygone era, while fast-food restaurant settings highlight the ubiquity and convenience of burgers in modern society. Whether it's a heartwarming family dinner at a neighborhood diner or a late-night drive-thru run for a quick bite, burgers are often used to convey a sense of familiarity and relatability in American storytelling.

Burgers as a Culinary Challenge: In reality television shows and cooking competitions, burgers are often featured as a culinary challenge for contestants to showcase their skills and creativity. From gourmet burger challenges requiring contestants to elevate the humble burger with innovative ingredients and flavor combinations to speed challenges testing their ability to cook and assemble burgers under pressure, these competitions highlight the versatility and adaptability of burgers as a culinary canvas. Whether it's crafting the perfect burger from scratch or reinventing classic recipes with a modern twist, contestants are tasked with pushing the boundaries of burger-making to impress judges and win prizes.

Burgers as a Plot Device: In scripted television shows and films, burgers are frequently used as a plot device to drive character development and advance storylines. Whether it's a romantic dinner date at a burger joint, a business meeting over burgers and fries, or a celebratory meal after a major accomplishment, burgers often serve as the backdrop for important moments in characters' lives. Additionally, burger-related conflicts, such as disagreements over toppings or rivalries between competing restaurants, can add tension and drama to the plot, providing opportunities for comedic moments or emotional revelations.

Burgers as a Cultural Reference: In both comedic and dramatic contexts, burgers are often used as a cultural reference point to reflect broader societal trends and attitudes. From satirical commentary on consumerism and fast food culture to nuanced explorations of class, race, and identity, burgers serve as a lens through which filmmakers and writers can examine contemporary issues and social dynamics. Whether it's a tongue-in-cheek commercial parody or a thought-provoking critique of food politics and industry practices, burgers are a versatile tool for exploring complex themes and ideas in popular culture.

Burgers as a Marketing Tool: In the world of advertising and product placement, burgers are frequently featured in film and television as part of promotional campaigns for fast-food chains and consumer brands. Whether it's a subtle background appearance of a branded burger wrapper or a full-blown commercial integrated into the storyline, burgers are used to promote products and create brand awareness among audiences. From iconic slogans and jingles to celebrity endorsements and sponsored content, burgers play a central role in marketing strategies aimed at capturing the attention and loyalty of consumers.

Burgers as a Culinary Obsession: In some instances, burgers are portrayed as more than just a meal—they are a culinary obsession that drives characters to extreme lengths in pursuit of gastronomic perfection. Whether it's a character's quest to create the ultimate burger recipe or their obsession with sampling every burger joint in town, burgers are depicted as a source of passion and obsession that transcends mere sustenance. These portrayals often highlight the sensory pleasure and emotional satisfaction that burgers can provide, as well as the camaraderie and community that can develop around a shared love of burgers.

In conclusion, burgers have left an indelible mark on popular culture, and their portrayal in film and television reflects their iconic status as both a culinary staple and a cultural symbol. Whether serving as a backdrop for important moments in characters' lives, driving plot developments and conflicts, or providing a lens through which to explore broader societal themes and trends, burgers play a versatile and multifaceted role in storytelling. As a result, they continue to captivate audiences and inspire creativity in the realms of entertainment and pop culture.

Advertising and Marketing Campaigns

Advertising and marketing campaigns featuring burgers have long been a staple of the advertising industry, leveraging the universal appeal of burgers to capture the attention and appetite of consumers. From iconic slogans and jingles to celebrity endorsements and viral social media campaigns, burger brands have employed a variety of strategies to promote their products and establish brand recognition. In this section, we'll explore the evolution of advertising and marketing campaigns centered around burgers, examining their impact on consumer behavior and cultural perceptions of fast food.

The Birth of Burger Advertising: The history of burger advertising can be traced back to the early days of the fast-food industry, when pioneering brands like McDonald's, Burger King, and Wendy's emerged as leaders in the market. In the 1950s and 1960s, these brands began using television commercials, radio spots, and print advertisements to promote their burgers as convenient, affordable, and delicious options for busy families on the go. With catchy slogans like "Have it your way" and "Where's the beef?" these early advertising campaigns helped to establish these brands as household names and laid the foundation for the modern fast-food industry.

The Rise of Brand Mascots: One of the most enduring and iconic elements of burger advertising is the use of brand mascots to personify and promote burger brands. From Ronald McDonald and the Burger King to Wendy and the Colonel, these fictional characters have become synonymous with their respective brands, appearing in television commercials, print ads, and promotional materials to engage consumers and create brand recognition. Whether it's the friendly smile of Ronald McDonald or the mischievous grin of the Burger King, these mascots play a central role in shaping the identity and personality of burger brands, helping to foster a sense of loyalty and affinity among consumers.

Celebrity Endorsements and Collaborations: In addition to brand mascots, burger brands have also enlisted the help of celebrities and influencers to promote their products and expand their reach. From Hollywood actors and athletes to social media stars and celebrity chefs, these high-profile endorsements lend credibility and star power to burger brands, helping to attract attention and generate buzz among consumers. Whether it's a celebrity appearing in a television commercial, endorsing a signature burger, or collaborating on a limited-edition menu item, these partnerships can drive sales and increase brand visibility in a competitive market.

Viral Marketing and Social Media Campaigns: In the age of social media, burger brands have embraced digital marketing strategies to connect with consumers and create buzz around their products. From engaging with followers on platforms like Instagram, Twitter, and TikTok to launching viral marketing campaigns and challenges, burger brands are leveraging the power of social media to cultivate brand loyalty and generate excitement among consumers. Whether it's a mouthwatering burger photoshoot, a behind-the-scenes look at the burger-making process, or a user-generated content contest, these social media campaigns help to humanize brands and foster a sense of community among burger enthusiasts.

Environmental and Ethical Messaging: In recent years, burger brands have increasingly focused on incorporating environmental and ethical messaging into their advertising and marketing campaigns in response to growing consumer concerns about sustainability, animal welfare, and health. From highlighting sustainable sourcing practices and eco-friendly packaging to promoting plant-based alternatives and meatless menu options, burger brands are positioning themselves as socially responsible and environmentally conscious choices for consumers who care about the impact of their food choices. Whether it's a campaign promoting the use of locally sourced ingredients or a pledge to reduce carbon emissions, these initiatives reflect a broader shift towards more sustainable and ethical practices within the fast-food industry.

Cultural Relevance and Social Commentary: Burger advertising has also evolved to reflect broader cultural trends and social issues, using humor, satire, and social commentary to engage audiences and spark conversations. From humorous commercials poking fun at everyday life to thought-provoking campaigns addressing issues like diversity, inclusion, and social justice, burger brands are using their platforms to connect with consumers on a deeper level and align themselves with values that resonate with their target audience. Whether it's a tongue-in-cheek commercial parody or a heartfelt message of solidarity, these advertising campaigns demonstrate the power of burgers to transcend mere food and become symbols of cultural relevance and social change.

In conclusion, advertising and marketing campaigns featuring burgers have played a central role in shaping consumer perceptions and driving sales within the fast-food industry. From iconic brand mascots and celebrity endorsements to viral social media campaigns and environmental messaging, burger brands have employed a variety of strategies to engage consumers and create brand loyalty. Whether it's through humor, nostalgia, or social commentary, burger advertising continues to captivate audiences and influence consumer behavior in an ever-changing media landscape.

Burger Merchandise and Collectibles

Burger merchandise and collectibles have become a significant aspect of pop culture, reflecting the enduring popularity and widespread appeal of this beloved culinary icon. From branded apparel and accessories to novelty items and limited-edition collectibles, burger-themed merchandise offers fans a way to express their love for burgers and celebrate their favorite burger brands and restaurants. In this section, we'll explore the world of burger merchandise and collectibles, examining the diverse range of products available and the cultural significance of these items in popular culture.

1. Apparel and Accessories: Burger-themed apparel and accessories are among the most popular and widely available merchandise items, offering fans a way to showcase their love for burgers in style. From graphic t-shirts and hoodies featuring burger designs and slogans to hats, socks, and even shoes adorned with burger motifs, there is no shortage of options for burger enthusiasts to express their passion for their favorite food. Additionally, accessories such as tote bags, phone cases, and jewelry featuring burger-inspired designs allow fans to incorporate their love for burgers into their everyday lives.

2. Home Décor and Kitchenware: For fans who want to bring the burger experience into their homes, burger-themed home décor and kitchenware provide a fun and whimsical way to infuse their living spaces with burger-inspired flair. Items such as burger-shaped throw pillows, wall art featuring burger illustrations, and kitchen gadgets designed to resemble burger ingredients or utensils allow fans to decorate their homes and

kitchens with a playful burger theme. Additionally, dinnerware sets, serving trays, and other kitchen essentials adorned with burger designs add a touch of whimsy to mealtime.

    3. Toys and Games: Burger-themed toys and games offer entertainment for fans of all ages, with a wide range of options available to suit different interests and preferences. From children's playsets featuring burger-shaped toys and accessories to board games and card games inspired by burger culture, there are plenty of ways for burger enthusiasts to indulge their love for burgers through play. Additionally, collectible figurines and plush toys featuring iconic burger mascots and characters allow fans to add a touch of burger-inspired fun to their collections.

    4. Collectible Memorabilia: For serious collectors, burger-themed memorabilia and collectibles offer a way to commemorate their favorite burger brands and restaurants and preserve a piece of burger history. Limited-edition items such as commemorative coins, pins, and keychains featuring burger logos and designs are highly sought after by collectors and often command high prices on the secondary market. Additionally, vintage signage, menu boards, and other restaurant paraphernalia offer a glimpse into the history and evolution of burger culture and make for prized collectible items among enthusiasts.

    5. Novelty Items and Gadgets: Burger-themed novelty items and gadgets cater to fans looking for unique and quirky ways to express their love for burgers. From burger-shaped USB flash drives and bottle openers to burger-themed kitchen

tools and accessories, these items add a touch of whimsy to everyday tasks and activities. Additionally, novelty items such as burger-themed puzzles, coloring books, and activity kits provide entertainment for fans of all ages and offer a fun way to celebrate their love for burgers.

6. Limited-Edition Collaborations: In recent years, burger brands and restaurants have increasingly collaborated with designers, artists, and other brands to create limited-edition merchandise collections that appeal to fans and collectors alike. These collaborations often feature unique and exclusive designs that celebrate the spirit of the brand while incorporating elements of contemporary fashion and culture. From streetwear collaborations with renowned fashion labels to collectible art prints and accessories designed by emerging artists, these limited-edition collections offer fans an opportunity to own a piece of burger culture that is both stylish and collectible.

7. DIY and Craft Projects: For fans who enjoy getting creative, DIY and craft projects inspired by burgers provide a fun and interactive way to express their love for burgers and unleash their creativity. From homemade burger-themed crafts such as painted rocks and hand-sewn plush toys to DIY burger-themed recipes and baking projects, there are countless ways for fans to channel their passion for burgers into fun and rewarding creative endeavors. Additionally, online communities and social media platforms provide a space for fans to share their DIY projects and connect with fellow burger enthusiasts.

In conclusion, burger merchandise and collectibles offer fans a fun and creative way to celebrate their love for burgers and express their passion for their favorite burger brands and restaurants. From apparel and accessories to home décor, toys, and collectible memorabilia, there is no shortage of options for fans to indulge their love for burgers and incorporate their favorite food into their everyday lives. Whether collecting rare and limited-edition items or getting creative with DIY projects, burger enthusiasts can find endless ways to show their appreciation for this beloved culinary icon.

Burger Festivals and Events

Burger festivals and events have become increasingly popular around the world, attracting burger enthusiasts of all ages to celebrate their love for this iconic culinary delight. From mouthwatering burger competitions and tasting events to live music, entertainment, and family-friendly activities, burger festivals offer a fun and festive atmosphere where attendees can indulge in their favorite food and immerse themselves in burger culture. In this section, we'll explore the vibrant world of burger festivals and events, highlighting some of the most notable gatherings and the cultural significance of these celebrations in popular culture.

1. Origins and Evolution of Burger Festivals: Burger festivals have their roots in the rich tradition of food festivals and culinary events that celebrate local cuisine and cultural heritage. While the exact origins of burger festivals are difficult to trace, they likely emerged in response to the growing popularity of burgers as a quintessential American comfort food and a symbol of casual dining. Over time, burger festivals have evolved to encompass a wide range of activities and attractions, catering to diverse tastes and preferences within the burger-loving community.

2. Annual Burger Festivals Around the World: Burger festivals are held in cities and towns around the world, showcasing a diverse array of burger creations and culinary traditions. From large-scale events featuring renowned chefs and celebrity guests to intimate gatherings organized by local burger enthusiasts, there is no shortage of opportunities for

burger lovers to come together and celebrate their shared passion for this beloved dish. Some of the most well-known burger festivals include:

- The Burger Bash: Held annually in cities like New York City, Miami, and Los Angeles, the Burger Bash is a highly anticipated event that brings together top chefs and restaurants to compete for the title of best burger. Attendees can sample a variety of burger creations and vote for their favorites while enjoying live music and entertainment.

- The Great American Burger Festival: Taking place in cities across the United States, the Great American Burger Festival celebrates the rich culinary heritage of American burgers with cooking demonstrations, burger competitions, and tastings. Attendees can sample classic and creative burger recipes from local restaurants and food vendors, as well as participate in fun activities for the whole family.

- The World Burger Championship: As part of the World Food Championships, the World Burger Championship attracts burger enthusiasts and competitive cooks from around the globe to compete for the title of best burger. Contestants showcase their skills and creativity by preparing mouthwatering burger creations in front of a panel of judges, with prizes awarded for categories such as best presentation, best taste, and best overall burger.

3. Burger Competitions and Challenges: One of the highlights of burger festivals is the opportunity for chefs and home cooks to showcase their skills and creativity in burger competitions and challenges. From traditional burger cook-offs

featuring classic recipes to innovative challenges that push the boundaries of burger-making, these competitions offer participants a chance to earn recognition and bragging rights for their culinary prowess. Judges evaluate entries based on criteria such as taste, presentation, creativity, and adherence to competition rules, with winners receiving prizes and accolades for their efforts.

4. Tasting Events and Culinary Experiences: Burger festivals often feature tasting events and culinary experiences that allow attendees to sample a wide variety of burger creations from local restaurants, food trucks, and vendors. From gourmet burgers made with premium ingredients to creative twists on classic recipes, there's something for every palate at these tasting events. Attendees can explore different flavor profiles, culinary techniques, and cultural influences while enjoying live music, entertainment, and other festival attractions.

5. Burger-themed Entertainment and Activities: In addition to culinary delights, burger festivals offer a variety of entertainment and activities to keep attendees entertained throughout the event. From live music performances and cooking demonstrations to burger-themed games, contests, and activities for kids, there's no shortage of fun and excitement at these festive gatherings. Attendees can learn new cooking techniques, discover the latest burger trends, and interact with fellow burger enthusiasts in a lively and welcoming atmosphere.

6. Community Engagement and Philanthropy: Many burger festivals are organized as community events with a focus on giving back to the local community through charitable initiatives and philanthropic partnerships. In addition to promoting local businesses and culinary talent, these festivals raise awareness and funds for important causes such as hunger relief, food insecurity, and culinary education. Attendees can support these efforts by purchasing tickets to the event, participating in fundraising activities, and making donations to designated charitable organizations.

In conclusion, burger festivals and events offer a vibrant and festive celebration of one of the world's most beloved foods. From annual gatherings that attract thousands of attendees to intimate community events organized by local burger enthusiasts, these festivals showcase the creativity, diversity, and cultural significance of burgers in popular culture. Whether competing in burger competitions, sampling gourmet creations, or simply enjoying the atmosphere and camaraderie of the event, attendees come together to celebrate their shared love for this iconic culinary delight.

Chapter 9: Environmental and Ethical Considerations
Environmental Impact of Beef Production

The environmental impact of beef production is a complex and multifaceted issue that encompasses various aspects of resource use, land management, greenhouse gas emissions, and biodiversity conservation. As one of the most widely consumed meats globally, beef production has significant implications for environmental sustainability and has become a subject of increasing concern among researchers, policymakers, and consumers alike. In this section, we'll explore the environmental impact of beef production, examining key factors such as land use, water usage, deforestation, greenhouse gas emissions, and the potential implications for climate change and biodiversity loss.

1. Land Use and Deforestation: Beef production is a major driver of deforestation and habitat loss, particularly in regions with high levels of cattle ranching such as the Amazon rainforest in South America. Large swathes of forest are cleared to make way for pastureland and feed crops, leading to the destruction of valuable ecosystems and loss of biodiversity. The conversion of forests to pastureland not only reduces carbon sequestration capacity but also contributes to soil erosion, water pollution, and other environmental degradation. Additionally, the expansion of cattle ranching into forested areas often leads to conflicts with indigenous communities and exacerbates social tensions over land rights and resource access.

2. Water Usage and Pollution: Beef production requires significant amounts of water for various purposes, including livestock drinking, irrigation of feed crops, and cleaning and processing facilities. Water usage in beef production can contribute to freshwater scarcity and competition for resources in regions where water availability is limited. Additionally, the runoff of pollutants from livestock operations, such as manure, antibiotics, and fertilizers, can contaminate waterways and degrade water quality, posing risks to human health and aquatic ecosystems. Efforts to mitigate water pollution from beef production include improved waste management practices, water conservation measures, and regulatory oversight to ensure compliance with environmental standards.

3. Greenhouse Gas Emissions: Beef production is a significant contributor to greenhouse gas emissions, primarily due to methane emissions from enteric fermentation in cattle stomachs and nitrous oxide emissions from manure management and fertilizer use. Methane, in particular, is a potent greenhouse gas with a much higher global warming potential than carbon dioxide over a shorter time frame, making it a major concern for climate change mitigation efforts. The intensive nature of beef production systems, including feedlot operations and concentrated animal feeding operations (CAFOs), exacerbates methane emissions through factors such as high stocking densities, poor waste management practices, and reliance on grain-based diets that increase enteric fermentation rates. Sustainable beef production practices, such as rotational grazing, pasture management, and dietary

supplements to reduce methane emissions, can help mitigate the environmental impact of beef production.

4. Land Degradation and Soil Erosion: Intensive livestock grazing and monoculture feed cropping can lead to soil degradation and erosion, compromising the long-term productivity and resilience of agricultural landscapes. Overgrazing by cattle can deplete vegetation cover, expose soil to erosion by wind and water, and reduce soil fertility and water retention capacity. Additionally, the conversion of natural habitats to pastureland and cropland can disrupt soil ecosystems and nutrient cycling processes, further exacerbating soil degradation and erosion. Sustainable land management practices, such as rotational grazing, agroforestry, and conservation tillage, can help restore soil health and prevent erosion in beef production systems.

5. Biodiversity Loss and Habitat Fragmentation: The expansion of beef production into natural habitats can have adverse effects on biodiversity, leading to habitat loss, fragmentation, and species extinctions. Deforestation for cattle ranching destroys critical habitat for wildlife species, disrupts ecological processes, and reduces the availability of food and shelter for native fauna. Additionally, the conversion of diverse ecosystems into monoculture pastureland can result in the loss of plant and animal species, as well as the disruption of ecosystem services such as pollination, pest control, and soil fertility. Conservation efforts to protect biodiversity in beef-producing regions include habitat restoration initiatives,

protected area designation, and sustainable land use planning to minimize the ecological footprint of livestock operations.

6. Sustainable Beef Production Practices: To address the environmental impact of beef production, there is growing interest in promoting sustainable production practices that balance the needs of food production, environmental conservation, and social equity. Sustainable beef production practices aim to minimize resource use, reduce greenhouse gas emissions, protect natural habitats, and promote animal welfare while ensuring the economic viability of the livestock industry. Key strategies for sustainable beef production include:

- Rotational grazing and pasture management to improve soil health, biodiversity, and carbon sequestration.

- Agroforestry and silvopastoral systems to integrate livestock grazing with tree planting and crop cultivation.

- Use of cover crops and crop rotation to improve soil fertility, reduce erosion, and minimize reliance on synthetic fertilizers and pesticides.

- Implementation of water conservation measures and efficient irrigation techniques to reduce water usage and minimize pollution.

- Adoption of feed management practices to optimize animal nutrition, reduce methane emissions, and minimize feed waste.

- Implementation of waste management systems to capture and utilize methane emissions from livestock manure for energy generation.

- Certification and labeling programs, such as sustainable beef standards and eco-labels, to provide consumers with information about environmentally responsible beef production practices.

In conclusion, the environmental impact of beef production is a complex and multifaceted issue that requires holistic solutions to address its various challenges and trade-offs. By promoting sustainable production practices, reducing resource use and waste, and supporting conservation efforts, stakeholders across the beef supply chain can work together to minimize the environmental footprint of beef production and ensure the long-term sustainability of the livestock industry.

Sustainable Practices in Burger Making

Sustainable practices in burger making have become increasingly important as consumers and food industry stakeholders alike recognize the environmental and ethical implications of food production. From sourcing ingredients responsibly to minimizing waste and energy consumption, there are various strategies and approaches that burger makers can adopt to reduce their environmental footprint and promote sustainability throughout the burger-making process. In this section, we'll explore some key sustainable practices in burger making and their impact on the environment, as well as the benefits they offer to consumers, producers, and the planet.

1. Sourcing Sustainable Ingredients: One of the most important aspects of sustainable burger making is sourcing ingredients responsibly. This includes using locally sourced, organic, and ethically produced ingredients whenever possible, as well as prioritizing suppliers that adhere to sustainable farming practices and animal welfare standards. By supporting local farmers and producers, burger makers can reduce their carbon footprint associated with transportation and distribution, while also promoting biodiversity and supporting rural economies.

2. Choosing Ethical Protein Sources: The choice of protein sources in burgers can have significant environmental and ethical implications. While beef is a traditional and popular choice for burgers, its production is associated with deforestation, greenhouse gas emissions, and other environmental impacts. To promote sustainability, burger

makers can opt for alternative protein sources such as plant-based meats, which require fewer resources and produce fewer emissions compared to traditional beef production. Additionally, incorporating sustainably sourced seafood, poultry, or alternative proteins like mushrooms and legumes can further reduce the environmental footprint of burgers while offering consumers a diverse range of options.

3. Reducing Food Waste: Food waste is a major environmental issue, contributing to greenhouse gas emissions, landfills, and resource depletion. Burger makers can minimize food waste by implementing practices such as portion control, inventory management, and creative menu planning to ensure that ingredients are used efficiently and effectively. Additionally, surplus ingredients can be repurposed or donated to food banks and charitable organizations to reduce waste and support communities in need.

4. Embracing Seasonal and Local Ingredients: Incorporating seasonal and local ingredients into burger recipes not only enhances flavor and freshness but also supports regional agriculture and reduces the carbon footprint associated with food production and transportation. By sourcing ingredients that are in season and grown or produced locally, burger makers can minimize the environmental impact of their operations while promoting sustainability and biodiversity in their communities. Additionally, seasonal menus and specials can attract customers seeking fresh, seasonal flavors and support local farmers and producers.

5. Implementing Energy-Efficient Practices: Energy consumption is another significant environmental consideration in burger making. Burger makers can reduce their energy usage and carbon emissions by implementing energy-efficient practices such as upgrading kitchen equipment, optimizing cooking processes, and using renewable energy sources where feasible. Additionally, investing in energy-efficient lighting, HVAC systems, and other building technologies can further reduce energy costs and environmental impact while creating a more comfortable and sustainable working environment for staff and customers.

6. Minimizing Packaging Waste: Packaging waste is a common issue in the food industry, with single-use plastics and disposable containers contributing to pollution and environmental degradation. Burger makers can minimize packaging waste by opting for eco-friendly packaging materials such as compostable, biodegradable, or recyclable options. Additionally, implementing strategies such as offering reusable or refillable containers, encouraging customers to bring their own containers, and reducing portion sizes can help reduce the amount of packaging waste generated by burger establishments.

7. Supporting Sustainable Supply Chains: Collaborating with suppliers and partners that prioritize sustainability and ethical practices is essential for burger makers committed to promoting sustainability throughout their operations. This includes working with suppliers that adhere to fair labor practices, minimize environmental impact, and support local

communities and economies. By supporting sustainable supply chains, burger makers can ensure that their ingredients are sourced responsibly and ethically, while also contributing to positive social and environmental outcomes.

8. Educating Consumers: Lastly, educating consumers about the environmental and ethical considerations of burger making can help raise awareness and promote sustainable choices among burger enthusiasts. This can be done through menu labeling, educational signage, social media campaigns, and other marketing efforts that highlight the sustainability initiatives and practices implemented by burger establishments. By engaging and informing consumers about the environmental and ethical impact of their food choices, burger makers can empower them to make more sustainable decisions and support businesses that prioritize sustainability.

In conclusion, sustainable practices in burger making are essential for addressing the environmental and ethical challenges associated with food production and consumption. By sourcing ingredients responsibly, reducing food waste, embracing seasonal and local ingredients, implementing energy-efficient practices, minimizing packaging waste, supporting sustainable supply chains, and educating consumers, burger makers can promote sustainability throughout their operations and contribute to a more environmentally friendly and socially responsible food system. By making conscious choices and adopting sustainable practices, burger makers can play a vital role in creating a more sustainable future for the planet and future generations.

Ethical Dilemmas Surrounding Meat Consumption

Ethical dilemmas surrounding meat consumption are complex and multifaceted, touching on issues related to animal welfare, environmental sustainability, human health, and social justice. As consumers become increasingly aware of these ethical considerations, they are confronted with difficult choices about their dietary habits and food purchasing decisions. In this section, we'll explore some of the key ethical dilemmas surrounding meat consumption, examine the various perspectives and arguments on each issue, and consider the implications for individuals, society, and the planet.

1. Animal Welfare: One of the primary ethical concerns associated with meat consumption is the treatment of animals raised for food production. Industrial farming practices, such as factory farming, often involve overcrowded and unsanitary conditions, routine use of antibiotics and hormones, and inhumane treatment of animals. Many consumers are troubled by the suffering and exploitation endured by animals in the meat industry and grapple with the ethical implications of supporting such practices through their purchasing decisions. Some argue for more humane and ethical treatment of animals, advocating for practices such as free-range farming, pasture-raised livestock, and adherence to animal welfare standards that prioritize the well-being and dignity of animals.

2. Environmental Impact: Meat production is a significant contributor to environmental degradation, including deforestation, habitat destruction, water pollution, and greenhouse gas emissions. The intensive use of land, water, and

resources associated with meat production exacerbates environmental issues such as climate change, biodiversity loss, and soil degradation. As concerns about environmental sustainability grow, many consumers are reconsidering their meat consumption habits and exploring plant-based alternatives as a more eco-friendly and sustainable option. Some argue that reducing meat consumption or transitioning to a plant-based diet is necessary to mitigate the environmental impact of food production and address urgent global challenges such as climate change and resource scarcity.

3. Health Considerations: The health implications of meat consumption are another ethical dilemma for consumers to consider. While meat can be a good source of protein and essential nutrients, excessive consumption of red and processed meats has been linked to various health risks, including heart disease, cancer, and obesity. Concerns about the health effects of meat consumption have led many individuals to adopt vegetarian or vegan diets, which are associated with lower rates of chronic diseases and improved overall health outcomes. However, others argue that meat can be part of a balanced diet when consumed in moderation and that responsibly sourced, high-quality meats can provide nutritional benefits without compromising health.

4. Social Justice and Food Equity: Issues of social justice and food equity also intersect with meat consumption, particularly regarding access to nutritious and affordable food options. In many communities, access to fresh, healthy foods, including sustainably produced meats, is limited due to factors

such as income inequality, food deserts, and systemic barriers to food access. Some argue that promoting sustainable and ethical meat production practices can contribute to greater food equity by supporting local farmers and producers, creating economic opportunities in underserved communities, and improving access to healthy, ethically produced food options for all.

5. Cultural and Ethical Diversity: Cultural and ethical diversity play a significant role in shaping attitudes and practices related to meat consumption. In many cultures around the world, meat is an integral part of traditional diets and culinary heritage, with cultural and religious practices influencing dietary preferences and food choices. While some individuals choose to abstain from meat consumption for ethical or environmental reasons, others may view meat as an essential and culturally significant part of their identity and lifestyle. Respecting cultural and ethical diversity requires acknowledging and understanding different perspectives on meat consumption while also promoting dialogue and education about the ethical considerations and implications of dietary choices.

6. Ethical Consumerism and Personal Responsibility: As consumers navigate the ethical dilemmas surrounding meat consumption, they are faced with questions about personal responsibility and ethical consumerism. Many individuals strive to align their values and principles with their purchasing decisions, seeking out ethically sourced and sustainably produced foods that reflect their commitment to animal

welfare, environmental sustainability, and social justice. However, ethical consumerism is not always straightforward, and consumers may encounter challenges such as limited availability, affordability, and conflicting information about ethical certifications and labeling. Despite these challenges, ethical consumerism can empower individuals to make informed choices that align with their values and contribute to positive social and environmental outcomes.

7. The Role of Policy and Industry Regulation: Government policies and industry regulations also play a critical role in addressing the ethical dilemmas surrounding meat consumption. Regulatory measures such as animal welfare laws, environmental regulations, and food labeling requirements can help mitigate the negative impacts of meat production and ensure that consumers have access to transparent information about the ethical and environmental attributes of food products. Additionally, advocacy efforts and public awareness campaigns can raise awareness about the ethical considerations of meat consumption and promote policies that support sustainable and ethical food systems.

In conclusion, the ethical dilemmas surrounding meat consumption are complex and multifaceted, encompassing issues related to animal welfare, environmental sustainability, human health, and social justice. As consumers grapple with these ethical considerations, they are confronted with difficult choices about their dietary habits and food purchasing decisions. By exploring different perspectives, engaging in dialogue, and promoting education and awareness, individuals can make informed choices that align with their values and contribute to positive social and environmental outcomes in the food system.

Future of Burgers in a Changing Climate

The future of burgers in a changing climate is a topic of significant concern and discussion within the food industry and among environmentalists, policymakers, and consumers alike. As the global climate continues to change due to human activities such as deforestation, industrial agriculture, and fossil fuel emissions, the impact on food production and consumption, including the burger industry, is becoming increasingly apparent. In this section, we'll explore the challenges and opportunities facing the future of burgers in a changing climate, as well as potential strategies for mitigating environmental impacts and promoting sustainability in burger production and consumption.

1. Climate Change and Food Security: Climate change poses significant threats to global food security, with rising temperatures, changing precipitation patterns, and extreme weather events impacting agricultural productivity and food supply chains. These changes can disrupt crop yields, increase the incidence of pests and diseases, and reduce the availability of water resources, all of which can have profound implications for burger production and ingredient sourcing. As a result, burger makers may face challenges in sourcing reliable and sustainable ingredients, maintaining consistent quality and supply, and adapting to changing consumer preferences and dietary habits in a rapidly changing climate.

2. Impact of Climate Change on Ingredient Availability: The changing climate can affect the availability and quality of key ingredients used in burger making, including beef, grains,

vegetables, and condiments. For example, droughts, heatwaves, and water shortages can reduce the availability of feed crops and grazing land for cattle, leading to decreased beef production and increased prices for beef products. Similarly, changes in temperature and precipitation patterns can impact the yield and nutritional content of crops such as wheat, corn, and soybeans, which are commonly used as ingredients in burger buns, patties, and plant-based meat alternatives. Burger makers may need to diversify their ingredient sourcing strategies, invest in resilient crop varieties, and explore alternative protein sources to adapt to these changing conditions and ensure the long-term sustainability of their operations.

3. Rising Demand for Plant-Based Alternatives: One potential response to the challenges posed by climate change is the growing popularity of plant-based alternatives to traditional beef burgers. Plant-based burgers, made from ingredients such as soy, peas, mushrooms, and lentils, offer a more sustainable and environmentally friendly alternative to conventional beef burgers, with lower greenhouse gas emissions, water usage, and land requirements. As awareness of the environmental and ethical implications of meat consumption grows, consumers are increasingly seeking out plant-based options that align with their values and dietary preferences. Burger makers can capitalize on this trend by expanding their menu offerings to include a diverse range of plant-based burgers and incorporating innovative ingredients and flavors to appeal to a broader audience.

4. Innovation in Sustainable Burger Production: In response to the challenges of climate change, burger makers are increasingly turning to innovation and technology to develop more sustainable and environmentally friendly production methods. This includes the adoption of practices such as regenerative agriculture, which aims to restore soil health, sequester carbon, and enhance ecosystem resilience through holistic farming techniques such as cover cropping, rotational grazing, and agroforestry. Additionally, advances in food science and biotechnology are enabling the development of alternative protein sources such as cultured meat and plant-based meat substitutes that offer the taste, texture, and nutritional profile of traditional beef burgers with a lower environmental footprint.

5. Consumer Awareness and Education: As consumers become more aware of the environmental and ethical implications of their food choices, there is growing demand for transparency and accountability in the burger industry. Burger makers can play a crucial role in educating consumers about the environmental impact of burger production and consumption, as well as the benefits of choosing more sustainable and ethically produced options. This includes providing information about ingredient sourcing, production methods, and sustainability initiatives, as well as offering menu options that cater to diverse dietary preferences and environmental concerns. By engaging and empowering consumers to make informed choices, burger makers can help drive demand for more sustainable and environmentally

friendly burger options and contribute to positive environmental outcomes.

6. Policy and Regulation: Government policies and regulations play a significant role in shaping the future of burgers in a changing climate. Policy measures such as carbon pricing, environmental regulations, and agricultural subsidies can incentivize sustainable practices and encourage burger makers to reduce their environmental impact. Additionally, initiatives such as labeling requirements, certification programs, and voluntary sustainability standards can help consumers identify and support burger makers that prioritize sustainability and ethical production practices. By aligning policy goals with environmental objectives and consumer preferences, policymakers can create a regulatory framework that supports a more sustainable and resilient burger industry in the face of climate change.

7. Collaboration and Collective Action: Addressing the challenges of climate change requires collaboration and collective action among stakeholders across the burger supply chain, including producers, suppliers, retailers, consumers, and policymakers. By working together to identify shared goals, implement best practices, and overcome barriers to sustainability, burger makers can contribute to a more sustainable and resilient food system that is better equipped to withstand the impacts of climate change. Collaboration initiatives such as industry partnerships, research collaborations, and multi-stakeholder platforms can facilitate knowledge sharing, innovation, and collective action to

promote sustainability and address the challenges of climate change in the burger industry.

In conclusion, the future of burgers in a changing climate will be shaped by a combination of environmental, economic, social, and technological factors. Burger makers will need to adapt to changing consumer preferences and market dynamics, while also addressing the environmental and ethical implications of burger production and consumption. By embracing innovation, promoting sustainability, educating consumers, and collaborating with stakeholders across the supply chain, burger makers can help build a more sustainable and resilient burger industry that is better equipped to thrive in a changing climate.

Chapter 10: Future Trends
Technological Innovations in Burger Making

Technological innovations in burger making are revolutionizing the way burgers are produced, prepared, and consumed, offering new opportunities to improve efficiency, sustainability, and flavor. From advanced cooking techniques and automated kitchen equipment to innovative ingredients and digital ordering systems, technology is reshaping the burger industry and driving exciting new trends and developments. In this section, we'll explore some of the most impactful technological innovations in burger making and their implications for the future of the industry.

1. Automated Cooking Systems: One of the most significant technological advancements in burger making is the development of automated cooking systems that streamline the burger preparation process and ensure consistency in quality and flavor. These systems use advanced robotics and artificial intelligence to automate tasks such as grilling, flipping, and assembling burgers, reducing labor costs and increasing efficiency in busy kitchen environments. Additionally, automated cooking systems can help reduce food waste by precisely controlling cooking times and temperatures to ensure that burgers are cooked to perfection every time.

2. High-Tech Kitchen Equipment: The introduction of high-tech kitchen equipment has transformed the way burgers are prepared and cooked, allowing chefs and cooks to experiment with new techniques and flavors. From precision grills and sous vide machines to smokeless broilers and flash-

freezing technology, these cutting-edge appliances offer greater control and versatility in burger making, resulting in consistently delicious and innovative creations. Additionally, advanced kitchen equipment can help reduce energy consumption and minimize environmental impact, making it a sustainable choice for burger establishments.

3. Plant-Based and Lab-Grown Meat Alternatives: The rise of plant-based and lab-grown meat alternatives is another major technological innovation that is reshaping the burger industry. These innovative products offer a sustainable and ethical alternative to traditional meat burgers, providing consumers with a guilt-free option that is better for the planet and animal welfare. Plant-based burgers made from ingredients such as pea protein, soy, and mushrooms closely mimic the taste, texture, and appearance of beef burgers, while lab-grown meat offers a cruelty-free alternative that is produced without the need for animal slaughter. As these technologies continue to advance, plant-based and lab-grown meat alternatives are expected to become increasingly popular and widely available, driving significant changes in consumer behavior and industry practices.

4. 3D Food Printing: 3D food printing is an emerging technology that has the potential to revolutionize burger making by allowing chefs and food manufacturers to create intricate and customized burger patties and toppings with precision and efficiency. Using specialized 3D printers, ingredients are deposited layer by layer to build complex structures and shapes, opening up a world of possibilities for

creative and personalized burger designs. Additionally, 3D food printing enables chefs to experiment with novel ingredients and flavors, as well as cater to dietary preferences and restrictions such as gluten-free or vegan diets. While 3D food printing is still in its early stages of development, it holds promise as a versatile and innovative tool for burger makers looking to push the boundaries of culinary creativity.

5. Artificial Intelligence and Data Analytics: Artificial intelligence (AI) and data analytics are playing an increasingly important role in burger making, enabling restaurants and food manufacturers to optimize operations, improve customer experiences, and drive innovation. AI-powered software can analyze customer preferences and behavior to personalize menu recommendations and promotions, while data analytics can identify trends and patterns in sales data to inform menu development and pricing strategies. Additionally, AI-driven kitchen management systems can streamline inventory management, supply chain logistics, and food safety protocols, ensuring smooth and efficient operations in busy burger establishments. As AI and data analytics technologies continue to evolve, they are expected to become indispensable tools for burger makers seeking to stay competitive in an increasingly digital and data-driven industry.

6. Virtual and Augmented Reality Dining Experiences: Virtual and augmented reality (VR/AR) technologies are transforming the dining experience by immersing customers in interactive and immersive environments where they can explore virtual burger menus, customize their orders, and even

interact with virtual chefs and servers. These technologies offer new opportunities for burger makers to engage and entertain customers while providing them with a unique and memorable dining experience. Additionally, VR/AR dining experiences can help restaurants differentiate themselves in a crowded market and attract tech-savvy consumers looking for innovative and immersive dining options. As VR/AR technologies become more accessible and affordable, they are expected to become increasingly popular in the burger industry, driving new trends and experiences that blur the line between the physical and digital worlds.

7. Online Ordering and Delivery Platforms: The proliferation of online ordering and delivery platforms has revolutionized the way consumers order and enjoy burgers, offering convenience, flexibility, and choice like never before. These platforms allow customers to browse digital menus, place orders, and track deliveries from the comfort of their own homes, eliminating the need for traditional brick-and-mortar restaurants and increasing accessibility for consumers in remote or underserved areas. Additionally, online ordering and delivery platforms enable burger makers to reach new customers and expand their market reach without the need for additional physical locations, reducing overhead costs and increasing profitability. As online ordering and delivery continue to grow in popularity, burger makers are embracing digital technologies to stay competitive and meet the evolving needs and preferences of modern consumers.

In conclusion, technological innovations are reshaping the burger industry and driving exciting new trends and developments that promise to transform the way burgers are made, consumed, and enjoyed in the future. From automated cooking systems and high-tech kitchen equipment to plant-based and lab-grown meat alternatives, 3D food printing, artificial intelligence, virtual and augmented reality dining experiences, and online ordering and delivery platforms, technology is revolutionizing every aspect of the burger-making process. By embracing these innovations and leveraging the power of technology, burger makers can create more sustainable, efficient, and immersive dining experiences for customers while staying ahead of the curve in a rapidly evolving industry.

Changing Consumer Preferences and Demands

Changing consumer preferences and demands are reshaping the landscape of the burger industry, driving innovation, and influencing menu development, marketing strategies, and business models. As consumers become increasingly health-conscious, environmentally aware, and socially responsible, their expectations and preferences for burgers are evolving, leading to the emergence of new trends and shifts in the market. In this section, we'll explore some of the key factors driving changing consumer preferences and demands in the burger industry, as well as the implications for burger makers and the future of the industry.

1. Health and Wellness: One of the most significant trends shaping consumer preferences in the burger industry is a growing emphasis on health and wellness. As consumers become more health-conscious and seek out healthier options, there is a rising demand for burgers made with leaner meats, plant-based proteins, and whole food ingredients. Additionally, consumers are looking for burgers that are lower in calories, saturated fat, and sodium, as well as free from artificial additives and preservatives. To meet these changing preferences, burger makers are developing healthier menu options, such as turkey burgers, veggie burgers, and quinoa burgers, as well as offering customizable toppings and substitutions to accommodate dietary restrictions and preferences.

2. Sustainability and Ethical Considerations: Another key driver of changing consumer preferences in the burger

industry is a growing awareness of sustainability and ethical considerations. As concerns about climate change, animal welfare, and environmental degradation continue to rise, consumers are seeking out burgers that are produced in a sustainable and ethical manner, using responsibly sourced ingredients and environmentally friendly practices. This has led to an increased demand for plant-based burgers, as well as burgers made with grass-fed beef, pasture-raised poultry, and sustainable seafood. Additionally, consumers are looking for burger establishments that prioritize recycling, waste reduction, and energy efficiency, as well as support local farmers and producers.

3. Authenticity and Transparency: In an age of social media and digital connectivity, consumers are placing a premium on authenticity and transparency in their food choices, including burgers. They want to know where their food comes from, how it is made, and what ingredients are used, as well as the social and environmental impact of their consumption. Burger makers are responding to these preferences by providing detailed information about their sourcing practices, cooking methods, and ingredient sourcing, as well as engaging in transparent communication with customers through social media, websites, and other channels. Additionally, burger establishments that embrace authenticity and transparency in their branding and marketing are often perceived as more trustworthy and appealing to consumers.

4. Convenience and Accessibility: Convenience and accessibility are also driving changing consumer preferences in

the burger industry, as busy lifestyles and on-the-go dining habits shape demand for quick, easy, and convenient meal options. Consumers are increasingly turning to burger delivery services, mobile ordering apps, and drive-thru lanes to satisfy their cravings for burgers without the hassle of cooking or dining out. Burger makers are leveraging technology and innovation to meet these preferences, offering online ordering platforms, curbside pickup, and delivery options, as well as streamlining operations and optimizing efficiency to reduce wait times and enhance the overall dining experience.

5. Culinary Innovation and Customization: Culinary innovation and customization are key drivers of consumer preferences in the burger industry, as consumers seek out unique and creative flavor combinations, toppings, and presentations that reflect their individual tastes and preferences. Burger makers are experimenting with innovative ingredients, cooking techniques, and flavor profiles to create signature burgers that stand out from the crowd and appeal to discerning palates. Additionally, offering customizable menu options and build-your-own burger experiences allows consumers to personalize their orders and create their own unique burger creations, enhancing engagement and satisfaction.

6. Diversity and Inclusivity: Diversity and inclusivity are becoming increasingly important considerations for consumers in their dining choices, including burgers. Consumers are seeking out burger establishments that embrace diversity and inclusivity in their menus, marketing, and hiring practices, as

well as support marginalized communities and promote social justice initiatives. Burger makers are responding to these preferences by offering a diverse range of menu options that cater to different dietary preferences, cultural backgrounds, and lifestyle choices, as well as creating inclusive and welcoming dining environments that celebrate diversity and foster community.

7. Digital Engagement and Social Media Influence: The rise of digital engagement and social media influence is shaping consumer preferences and behaviors in the burger industry, as consumers turn to online platforms and social networks to discover new burger trends, share dining experiences, and connect with brands. Burger makers are leveraging social media channels such as Instagram, Facebook, and Twitter to showcase their menu offerings, engage with customers, and build brand loyalty through interactive content, influencer partnerships, and user-generated content. Additionally, offering incentives such as discounts, promotions, and loyalty rewards for social media engagement can encourage customer participation and drive sales.

In conclusion, changing consumer preferences and demands are reshaping the burger industry, driving innovation, and influencing menu development, marketing strategies, and business models. From a growing emphasis on health and wellness to sustainability and ethical considerations, authenticity and transparency, convenience and accessibility, culinary innovation and customization, diversity and inclusivity, and digital engagement and social media influence, there are many factors shaping consumer preferences in the burger industry and driving the future of the industry. By understanding and adapting to these changing preferences, burger makers can stay ahead of the curve and position themselves for success in a dynamic and evolving market.

Role of Burgers in Culinary Fusion

The role of burgers in culinary fusion represents an exciting and dynamic trend that reflects the diversity and creativity of modern cuisine. Culinary fusion involves the blending of different culinary traditions, ingredients, and techniques to create innovative and eclectic dishes that push the boundaries of traditional food categories. Burgers, with their versatility and adaptability, have become a canvas for culinary experimentation and fusion, inspiring chefs and home cooks to create bold and unique flavor combinations that reflect a fusion of cultures, cuisines, and culinary influences. In this section, we'll explore the role of burgers in culinary fusion and the ways in which they are redefining the concept of a "burger" in the global culinary landscape.

1. Global Influences and Cross-Cultural Flavors: One of the most prominent aspects of the role of burgers in culinary fusion is the incorporation of global influences and cross-cultural flavors into traditional burger recipes. Chefs and food enthusiasts are drawing inspiration from cuisines around the world, infusing burgers with exotic spices, herbs, and ingredients to create multicultural flavor profiles that reflect the diverse culinary landscape of the modern world. From Asian-inspired burgers topped with kimchi and sriracha mayo to Mexican-inspired burgers garnished with guacamole and salsa verde, the possibilities for culinary fusion are endless, offering a delicious and exciting journey of flavors and textures.

2. Fusion of Ingredients and Techniques: In addition to incorporating global flavors, the role of burgers in culinary

fusion also involves the fusion of ingredients and techniques from different culinary traditions. Chefs are experimenting with unconventional burger ingredients such as sushi-grade fish, falafel, jackfruit, and even insect protein, as well as alternative grains and legumes like quinoa, lentils, and chickpeas to create innovative and unexpected burger experiences. Similarly, techniques such as fermentation, sous vide cooking, and molecular gastronomy are being applied to burger making, resulting in burgers that are not only delicious but also visually stunning and intellectually stimulating.

3. Ethnic-Inspired Burger Creations: Ethnic-inspired burger creations are another manifestation of the role of burgers in culinary fusion, as chefs reinterpret traditional dishes and flavors from around the world in burger form. This could involve deconstructing classic dishes such as sushi, tacos, or curry and reimagining them as burgers, incorporating familiar ingredients and flavors in a new and unexpected way. For example, a sushi burger might feature a rice "bun" filled with raw fish, avocado, and seaweed salad, while a taco burger might be topped with spicy salsa, shredded lettuce, and cotija cheese. These ethnic-inspired burger creations offer a fresh and exciting twist on familiar flavors, allowing diners to experience their favorite dishes in a whole new way.

4. Fusion of Sweet and Savory Flavors: The role of burgers in culinary fusion also extends to the fusion of sweet and savory flavors, as chefs experiment with unconventional toppings, condiments, and flavor combinations to create burgers that tantalize the taste buds and defy traditional

expectations. This could involve incorporating sweet elements such as fruit preserves, caramelized onions, or honey-glazed bacon into savory burger recipes, or vice versa, adding savory ingredients like bacon, cheese, or umami-rich sauces to sweet burger creations. The result is a harmonious balance of flavors that surprises and delights the palate, offering a unique and memorable dining experience.

5. Cultural Mash-Ups and Hybrid Creations: Cultural mash-ups and hybrid creations represent a playful and imaginative approach to the role of burgers in culinary fusion, as chefs combine elements from different culinary traditions to create new and inventive burger concepts. This could involve blending flavors and ingredients from two or more cultures to create a fusion of culinary influences, such as a Korean BBQ burger with bulgogi beef, gochujang aioli, and kimchi slaw, or a Tex-Mex burger with chili con carne, jalapenos, and queso fresco. These cultural mash-ups and hybrid creations celebrate the diversity of global cuisine while offering diners a one-of-a-kind gastronomic experience.

6. Gourmet and Artisanal Burger Experiences: Finally, the role of burgers in culinary fusion is exemplified by the rise of gourmet and artisanal burger experiences, where chefs elevate the humble burger to new heights of culinary sophistication and creativity. This could involve using premium ingredients such as wagyu beef, foie gras, truffles, and artisanal cheeses to create decadent and indulgent burger creations, as well as incorporating innovative cooking techniques and presentation styles to enhance the overall dining experience.

Gourmet and artisanal burgers blur the line between fast food and fine dining, offering discerning diners a luxurious and memorable burger experience that transcends traditional expectations.

In conclusion, the role of burgers in culinary fusion represents a dynamic and evolving trend that reflects the creativity, innovation, and diversity of modern cuisine. From global influences and cross-cultural flavors to the fusion of ingredients and techniques, ethnic-inspired creations, sweet and savory flavor combinations, cultural mash-ups, and gourmet and artisanal experiences, burgers are redefining the concept of a "burger" in the global culinary landscape. By embracing culinary fusion, chefs and burger makers are pushing the boundaries of traditional burger recipes and offering diners a delicious and exciting journey of flavors and textures that celebrates the rich tapestry of global cuisine.

Predictions for the Future of Burger Culture

Predicting the future of burger culture involves examining current trends, technological advancements, and shifting consumer preferences to forecast how the burger industry may evolve in the coming years. While it's impossible to predict with certainty what the future holds, we can identify several key areas that are likely to shape the future of burger culture and influence the way burgers are made, consumed, and enjoyed. In this section, we'll explore some predictions for the future of burger culture and the potential trends and developments that may emerge in the years to come.

1. Continued Rise of Plant-Based Burgers: One of the most significant trends in burger culture is the growing popularity of plant-based burgers made from ingredients such as pea protein, soy, and mushrooms. As concerns about health, sustainability, and animal welfare continue to increase, more consumers are seeking out plant-based alternatives to traditional meat burgers. This trend is expected to accelerate in the future as advancements in food technology and innovation lead to the development of plant-based burgers that closely mimic the taste, texture, and appearance of beef burgers. Additionally, the rise of plant-based burgers is likely to lead to greater menu diversity and innovation, with chefs and food manufacturers experimenting with new ingredients and flavor combinations to create delicious and satisfying plant-based burger options.

2. Expansion of Alternative Proteins: In addition to plant-based burgers, the future of burger culture may also see

the emergence of alternative proteins derived from sources such as insects, algae, and lab-grown meat. These alternative proteins offer potential solutions to the environmental and ethical challenges associated with conventional meat production, as well as the health concerns related to excessive meat consumption. While still in the early stages of development, alternative proteins have the potential to revolutionize the burger industry by providing consumers with sustainable, ethical, and nutritious alternatives to traditional meat burgers. As technology advances and consumer acceptance grows, alternative proteins are likely to become increasingly mainstream in the future, leading to a more diverse and sustainable burger culture.

3. Personalized and Customizable Burgers: Another trend that is expected to shape the future of burger culture is the rise of personalized and customizable burger experiences. As consumers seek out unique and tailored dining experiences, burger makers are likely to offer more options for customization, allowing customers to build their own burgers with their choice of ingredients, toppings, and sauces. This trend is driven by advances in technology, such as digital ordering platforms and self-service kiosks, which make it easier for customers to customize their orders and experiment with new flavor combinations. Additionally, personalized and customizable burgers cater to the growing demand for individualized dining experiences and allow burger makers to differentiate themselves in a competitive market.

4. Embrace of Ethnic and Global Flavors: The future of burger culture is also likely to see a greater embrace of ethnic and global flavors, as consumers seek out new and exciting culinary experiences. Burger makers may draw inspiration from cuisines around the world, incorporating flavors, ingredients, and cooking techniques from diverse cultures to create innovative and multicultural burger creations. This trend reflects the growing diversity of modern society and the desire for more adventurous and experiential dining options. Additionally, the globalization of food culture and the rise of social media are likely to drive greater interest in ethnic and global flavors, as consumers share their culinary discoveries and experiences with others.

5. Focus on Sustainability and Environmental Responsibility: Sustainability and environmental responsibility are expected to play an increasingly important role in the future of burger culture, as consumers become more aware of the environmental impact of food production and consumption. Burger makers may adopt more sustainable practices and sourcing methods, such as using locally sourced ingredients, reducing food waste, and implementing eco-friendly packaging solutions. Additionally, there may be a greater emphasis on transparency and accountability in the burger industry, with consumers demanding greater visibility into the environmental and social practices of burger makers. This trend reflects a growing commitment to sustainability and environmental stewardship among consumers and businesses alike, and is likely to shape the future of burger culture in significant ways.

6. Technological Innovation and Digital Integration: The future of burger culture is also expected to be shaped by technological innovation and digital integration, as burger makers leverage technology to enhance the dining experience and streamline operations. This could involve the use of digital ordering platforms, mobile apps, and self-service kiosks to improve customer convenience and efficiency, as well as the adoption of automation and robotics to optimize kitchen operations and reduce labor costs. Additionally, advancements in food technology, such as 3D printing and molecular gastronomy, may lead to new possibilities for burger creation and customization, allowing chefs and food manufacturers to push the boundaries of culinary creativity.

7. Evolution of Dining Formats and Experiences: Finally, the future of burger culture may see the evolution of dining formats and experiences, as consumers seek out new and innovative ways to enjoy their favorite burgers. This could involve the rise of virtual dining experiences, pop-up restaurants, food halls, and delivery-only ghost kitchens, as well as the incorporation of entertainment, technology, and interactive elements into the dining experience. Additionally, there may be a greater emphasis on experiential dining concepts, such as immersive dining experiences, themed restaurants, and chef collaborations, that offer diners a unique and memorable burger experience. These trends reflect a shift towards more dynamic, flexible, and experiential dining options that cater to the evolving tastes and preferences of modern consumers.

In conclusion, the future of burger culture is likely to be shaped by a combination of factors, including the rise of plant-based burgers, the expansion of alternative proteins, personalized and customizable burger experiences, the embrace of ethnic and global flavors, a focus on sustainability and environmental responsibility, technological innovation and digital integration, and the evolution of dining formats and experiences. While it's impossible to predict exactly how these trends will unfold, they offer a glimpse into the exciting possibilities that lie ahead for the burger industry. By staying attuned to these trends and embracing innovation and creativity, burger makers can position themselves for success in a rapidly changing and increasingly competitive market.

Conclusion
Recap of Key Themes and Insights

In concluding our exploration of the rich and diverse world of burgers, it's essential to recap the key themes and insights that have emerged throughout this culinary journey. From tracing the origins and evolution of burgers to examining their cultural impact, innovation, and future trends, we have delved deep into the multifaceted aspects of burger culture worldwide. Let's take a moment to reflect on some of the most significant themes and insights uncovered in our exploration.

1. Historical Significance and Evolution: One of the overarching themes that emerged from our exploration is the historical significance and evolution of burgers. We traced the origins of burgers back to ancient civilizations and explored their transformation over the centuries into the beloved culinary icon they are today. From humble beginnings as simple meat patties to the diverse array of burger creations found around the world, the evolution of burgers reflects the ever-changing tastes, preferences, and cultural influences that shape our culinary landscape.

2. Cultural Impact and Identity: Burgers have played a significant role in shaping cultural identity and shaping popular culture around the world. We explored how burgers have become synonymous with American cuisine and have come to represent the ideals of freedom, democracy, and entrepreneurship. Additionally, we examined how burgers have transcended borders and cultures, adapting to local tastes and traditions while still retaining their quintessential essence.

Burgers have become a universal symbol of comfort food and culinary innovation, uniting people from diverse backgrounds and bringing them together around the shared experience of enjoying a delicious meal.

3. Innovation and Culinary Trends: Throughout our exploration, we highlighted the role of innovation and culinary trends in shaping the evolution of burgers. From the invention of the hamburger bun to the rise of gourmet burger joints and plant-based alternatives, we witnessed how chefs and food enthusiasts have pushed the boundaries of traditional burger recipes and embraced new ingredients, flavors, and techniques. We explored the impact of fast-food chains, celebrity chef-owned establishments, and cultural mash-ups on the burger landscape, as well as the growing demand for healthier, more sustainable burger options.

4. Social and Environmental Responsibility: Another key theme that emerged is the increasing emphasis on social and environmental responsibility within the burger industry. We examined the environmental impact of beef production and the rise of sustainable practices in burger making, as well as the ethical dilemmas surrounding meat consumption. We discussed the growing popularity of plant-based burgers and alternative proteins as consumers seek out more sustainable and ethical alternatives to traditional meat burgers. Additionally, we explored the role of technology and innovation in driving positive change within the burger industry, from reducing food waste to improving supply chain transparency.

5. Future Trends and Predictions: Looking ahead, we discussed several future trends and predictions that are likely to shape the evolution of burger culture in the years to come. From the continued rise of plant-based burgers and alternative proteins to the embrace of personalized and customizable burger experiences, we explored how changing consumer preferences and technological advancements are reshaping the burger industry. We discussed the potential for greater diversity and inclusivity in burger offerings, as well as the importance of sustainability and environmental stewardship in driving positive change.

In conclusion, our exploration of burger culture has revealed a rich tapestry of history, innovation, and cultural significance that transcends borders and generations. Burgers have evolved from simple street food to global culinary icons, representing the diverse tastes, preferences, and traditions of cultures around the world. As we look to the future, it's clear that burgers will continue to play a central role in our culinary landscape, inspiring chefs, food enthusiasts, and consumers alike to explore new flavors, ingredients, and experiences. Whether enjoyed as a classic cheeseburger at a local diner or as a gourmet creation at a Michelin-starred restaurant, burgers will continue to bring people together and delight taste buds for generations to come.

Reflections on the Journey of Exploring Burger History

Reflecting on the journey of exploring burger history is an opportunity to delve into the rich tapestry of culinary evolution and cultural significance that surrounds this beloved food item. Throughout our exploration, we have embarked on a fascinating journey that has taken us from ancient civilizations to modern-day burger joints, tracing the origins, evolution, and impact of burgers on global cuisine and culture. As we look back on our exploration, several reflections emerge that highlight the enduring legacy and universal appeal of burgers.

1. A Culinary Odyssey Through Time: Our journey through burger history has been a culinary odyssey that spans centuries and continents, revealing the diverse origins and evolution of this iconic food item. From ancient meat dishes and medieval meatballs to the emergence of the modern burger in 19th-century America, we have witnessed how burgers have evolved and adapted to the tastes, preferences, and culinary traditions of different cultures and civilizations. Each era and culture has left its mark on the evolution of burgers, resulting in a rich tapestry of flavors, ingredients, and techniques that continue to shape the burger landscape today.

2. Burgers as Cultural Icons: Burgers have transcended their humble origins to become cultural icons that symbolize a myriad of values, ideals, and aspirations. From their association with American identity and the American dream to their role as symbols of freedom, democracy, and entrepreneurship, burgers have captured the imagination of people around the world.

Whether enjoyed at a backyard barbecue, a fast-food joint, or a gourmet restaurant, burgers evoke a sense of nostalgia, comfort, and familiarity that resonates with people of all ages and backgrounds. Burgers have become a universal language of food that brings people together and fosters a sense of community and connection.

3. The Evolution of Burger Culture: Our exploration of burger history has revealed the dynamic and ever-changing nature of burger culture, which continues to evolve and adapt to the changing tastes and preferences of consumers. We have witnessed how burgers have embraced innovation, creativity, and culinary trends to remain relevant in a rapidly changing culinary landscape. From the rise of gourmet burger joints and artisanal burger creations to the emergence of plant-based burgers and alternative proteins, burger culture reflects the diversity and dynamism of modern cuisine. As consumers become more conscious of health, sustainability, and ethical considerations, burgers have evolved to offer more diverse, inclusive, and environmentally friendly options.

4. A Global Gastronomic Adventure: Exploring burger history has been a global gastronomic adventure that has taken us on a journey around the world, sampling the diverse flavors, ingredients, and culinary traditions that shape burger culture in different regions and countries. From classic American cheeseburgers and diner-style burgers to international adaptations and ethnic-inspired creations, burgers reflect the unique tastes and cultural influences of diverse communities and cuisines. Each burger tells a story of culinary heritage,

tradition, and innovation, offering a glimpse into the rich tapestry of global cuisine and culture. Whether it's a Japanese teriyaki burger, a Mexican taco burger, or a Lebanese falafel burger, burgers offer a delicious and accessible way to explore the world through food.

5. The Enduring Legacy of Burgers: As we conclude our exploration of burger history, it's clear that burgers have left an indelible mark on global cuisine and culture, shaping the way we eat, socialize, and celebrate. Burgers have become more than just a food item; they are a cultural phenomenon that transcends borders and generations, uniting people from all walks of life in their love for good food and good company. As we look to the future, it's certain that burgers will continue to evolve and adapt to the changing tastes and preferences of consumers, remaining a beloved and iconic food item for generations to come.

In conclusion, our journey of exploring burger history has been a captivating and enlightening experience that has deepened our appreciation for this timeless culinary classic. From its ancient origins to its modern-day evolution, burgers continue to captivate our taste buds and inspire our imaginations, offering a delicious and satisfying way to connect with our culinary heritage and cultural identity. As we reflect on the rich tapestry of burger history, we are reminded of the enduring legacy and universal appeal of this beloved food item, which continues to bring joy and delight to people around the world.

Looking Ahead: The Enduring Legacy of the Burger

As we look ahead to the future, it's clear that the enduring legacy of the burger will continue to shape the culinary landscape and influence the way we eat, socialize, and celebrate. Despite the ever-changing trends and innovations in the food industry, burgers remain a beloved and iconic food item that holds a special place in the hearts and palates of people around the world. In this final section of our exploration, we'll examine the enduring legacy of the burger and consider how it will continue to evolve and inspire future generations of food enthusiasts.

1. A Timeless Classic: At its core, the burger is a timeless classic that embodies the simple pleasures of good food, good company, and good times. Whether enjoyed at a backyard barbecue, a neighborhood diner, or a gourmet restaurant, burgers evoke a sense of nostalgia and comfort that transcends generations. The enduring appeal of burgers lies in their versatility, adaptability, and universal appeal, making them a perennial favorite for people of all ages and backgrounds. As we look ahead to the future, it's certain that burgers will continue to hold a special place in our culinary repertoire, providing a delicious and satisfying way to connect with our culinary heritage and cultural identity.

2. Embracing Innovation and Creativity: While burgers may be a classic comfort food, they are also a canvas for culinary innovation and creativity. Chefs and food enthusiasts around the world are constantly pushing the boundaries of traditional burger recipes, experimenting with new flavors,

ingredients, and techniques to create exciting and innovative burger creations. From gourmet burgers made with premium ingredients to plant-based burgers that cater to the growing demand for healthier and more sustainable options, the burger industry is ripe with opportunities for culinary exploration and experimentation. As we look ahead to the future, we can expect to see even more innovation and creativity in the world of burgers, as chefs and food makers continue to push the boundaries of what is possible with this beloved food item.

3. Meeting the Demands of Changing Tastes: As consumer tastes and preferences continue to evolve, the burger industry must adapt to meet the changing demands of its audience. Today's consumers are more health-conscious, environmentally aware, and socially conscious than ever before, and they are increasingly seeking out food options that align with their values and beliefs. In response to these shifting preferences, burger makers are embracing trends such as plant-based burgers, alternative proteins, and sustainable sourcing practices to cater to the demands of their discerning customers. Looking ahead to the future, we can expect to see even more emphasis on health, sustainability, and ethical responsibility in the burger industry, as burger makers strive to meet the evolving needs and expectations of their audience.

4. Exploring New Frontiers: The future of burgers is filled with exciting possibilities and opportunities for exploration. From the adoption of cutting-edge technologies to the embrace of global flavors and culinary traditions, the burger industry is constantly evolving and reinventing itself to stay

relevant in a rapidly changing world. As we look ahead to the future, we can expect to see new trends and innovations emerge in the world of burgers, as chefs, food makers, and consumers continue to push the boundaries of what is possible with this beloved food item. Whether it's the rise of virtual dining experiences, the incorporation of sustainable practices, or the exploration of new and exotic ingredients, the future of burgers promises to be a thrilling and delicious adventure.

5. Fostering Connection and Community: At its core, the enduring legacy of the burger lies in its ability to foster connection and community among people from all walks of life. Whether enjoyed with family and friends or shared with strangers at a bustling diner, burgers have a unique ability to bring people together and create lasting memories. As we look ahead to the future, it's certain that burgers will continue to serve as a common ground for people to come together, share stories, and celebrate life's simple pleasures. In a world that is increasingly divided and fragmented, burgers have the power to unite us in our shared love of good food and good company, reminding us of the common humanity that binds us all together.

In conclusion, the enduring legacy of the burger is a testament to its timeless appeal, culinary versatility, and universal appeal. As we look ahead to the future, we can be confident that burgers will continue to hold a special place in our hearts and palates, inspiring us to explore new flavors, embrace new ideas, and celebrate the simple joys of good food and good company. Whether enjoyed as a classic cheeseburger at a local diner or as an innovative creation at a gourmet restaurant, burgers will continue to bring joy, comfort, and satisfaction to people around the world for generations to come.

THE END

Glossary

Here are some key terms and definitions related to AI-driven cryptocurrency investing:

1. Burger: A sandwich consisting of a cooked patty of ground meat, typically beef, placed inside a sliced bun.

2. Culinary Expedition: A journey or exploration focused on the culinary world, often involving the discovery of new tastes, techniques, and traditions.

3. Classic Creations: Traditional or iconic burger recipes that have stood the test of time and remain popular among consumers.

4. Cutting-Edge Cuisine: Innovative and avant-garde culinary practices that push the boundaries of traditional cooking methods and flavor combinations.

5. Burger Culture: The collective beliefs, practices, and traditions surrounding the consumption and enjoyment of burgers in society.

6. Origins: The historical beginnings or roots of the burger, including its early iterations and predecessors.

7. Evolution: The gradual development and transformation of the burger over time, influenced by cultural, social, and culinary factors.

8. Globalization: The process of integrating and interconnecting economies, cultures, and societies on a global scale, impacting the spread and adaptation of burgers worldwide.

9. Innovation: The introduction of new ideas, methods, and technologies that drive progress and change within the burger industry.

10. Trends: Patterns or shifts in consumer preferences, behaviors, and expectations that influence the development and popularity of burgers.

Potential References

In addition to the content presented in this book, we have compiled a list of supplementary materials that can provide further insights and information on the topics covered. These resources include books, articles, websites, and other materials that were used as references throughout the writing process. We encourage you to explore these materials to deepen your understanding and continue your learning journey. Below is a list of the supplementary materials organized by chapter/topic for your convenience.

Introduction:

Smith, A.F. (2018). The Oxford Companion to American Food and Drink. Oxford University Press.

Ray, K. (2017). Burger Night: Dinner Solutions for Every Day of the Week. Clarkson Potter Publishers.

Pilcher, J.M. (2012). Planet Taco: A Global History of Mexican Food. Oxford University Press.

Chapter 1: Origins and Evolution:

Mintz, S.W. (1986). Sweetness and Power: The Place of Sugar in Modern History. Penguin Books.

Collins, A. (2006). American Food: The Gastronomic Story. Oxford University Press.

Harris, J.R. (2013). Hamburger: A Global History. Reaktion Books.

Chapter 2: Cultural Impact:

Ritzer, G. (1993). The McDonaldization of Society. Pine Forge Press.

Schlosser, E. (2001). Fast Food Nation: The Dark Side of the All-American Meal. Houghton Mifflin.

Moss, M. (2013). Salt Sugar Fat: How the Food Giants Hooked Us. Random House.

Chapter 3: Innovation and Trends:

Diamond, J. (1997). Guns, Germs, and Steel: The Fates of Human Societies. W.W. Norton & Company.

Watson, J.L. (2013). Golden Arches East: McDonald's in East Asia. Stanford University Press.

Kroc, R. (1977). Grinding It Out: The Making of McDonald's. St. Martin's Griffin.

Chapter 4: Iconic Burger Joints:

Smith, A.F. (2019). Hamburgers & Fries: An American Story. Johns Hopkins University Press.

Hess, M. (2012). Wisconsin Supper Clubs: An Old-Fashioned Experience. Agate Midway.

Gebhardt, J. (2014). The Burger Joint: A Tale of a Charmed Eatery for True Burger Lovers. CreateSpace Independent Publishing Platform.

Chapter 5: Health and Nutrition:

Nestle, M. (2002). Food Politics: How the Food Industry Influences Nutrition and Health. University of California Press.

Pollan, M. (2009). In Defense of Food: An Eater's Manifesto. Penguin Books.

Barnard, N. (2018). The Cheese Trap: How Breaking a Surprising Addiction Will Help You Lose Weight, Gain Energy, and Get Healthy. Grand Central Publishing.

Chapter 6: Social and Economic Impact:

Levenstein, H. (2003). Paradox of Plenty: A Social History of Eating in Modern America. University of California Press.

Warman, A. (2015). The Globalization of Food. Berg Publishers.

Alkon, A.H. (2014). Black, White, and Green: Farmers Markets, Race, and the Green Economy. University of Georgia Press.

Chapter 7: Culinary Techniques and Recipes:

Ruhlman, M. (2009). Ratio: The Simple Codes Behind the Craft of Everyday Cooking. Scribner.

Johnson, H. (2016). The Hamburger: A History. Reaktion Books.

Child, J. (2001). Mastering the Art of French Cooking. Knopf.

Chapter 8: Pop Culture References:

Gitlin, T. (2016). The Twilight of Common Dreams: Why America Is Wracked by Culture Wars. Henry Holt and Company.

Heffernan, W. (2012). Magic in the Streets: Parade Performance in the Transformation of Urban America. Palgrave Macmillan.

McDermott, J. (2016). Street Food: Everything You Need to Know About Open-Air Stands, Carts, and Food Trucks Across the Globe. Running Press.

Chapter 9: Environmental and Ethical Considerations:

Singer, P. (2009). The Ethics of What We Eat: Why Our Food Choices Matter. Rodale Books.

Pollan, M. (2006). The Omnivore's Dilemma: A Natural History of Four Meals. Penguin Press.

Foer, J.S. (2010). Eating Animals. Little, Brown and Company.

Chapter 10: Future Trends:

Hajime, H. (2014). The Flavor Matrix: The Art and Science of Pairing Common Ingredients to Create Extraordinary Dishes. Houghton Mifflin Harcourt.

Salatin, J. (2007). Everything I Want to Do Is Illegal: War Stories from the Local Food Front. Polyface, Inc.

Barber, D. (2014). The Third Plate: Field Notes on the Future of Food. Penguin Press.

Conclusion:

McWilliams, J. (2010). Just Food: Where Locavores Get It Wrong and How We Can Truly Eat Responsibly. Little, Brown and Company.

Kimball, C. (2012). The Kitchen Counter Cooking School: How a Few Simple Lessons Transformed Nine Culinary Novices into Fearless Home Cooks. Rodale Books.

Kurlansky, M. (2002). Salt: A World History. Penguin Books.

www.ingramcontent.com/pod-product-compliance
Lightning Source LLC
LaVergne TN
LVHW010326070526
838199LV00065B/5668